D1432828

ON THE HISTORY OF PHILOSOPHY

ON THE HISTORY
OF
PHILOSOPHY
and other essays

BY

FREDERICK COPLESTON, S.J., F.B.A.

*Professor Emeritus of History of Philosophy
in the University of London*

SEARCH PRESS LONDON

BARNES & NOBLE BOOKS NEW YORK
(a division of Harper & Row Publishers, Inc.)

SEARCH PRESS LIMITED
2−10 Jerdan Place, London SW6 5PT
Great Britain
First published 1979
Copyright ©Frederick Copleston 1979
ISBN 0 85532 371 X

Published in the USA 1979 by
Harper & Row Publishers, Inc.
BARNES & NOBLE IMPORT DIVISION

ISBN 0 06 491285 X

SETTING BY �-ART, CROYDON, SURREY
PRINTED AND BOUND IN GREAT BRITAIN BY
BILLING & SONS LTD, GUILDFORD, LONDON & WORCESTER

90
.786
979

CONTENTS

PREFACE

Apart from the third and fifth chapters, the essays contained in this collection have not hitherto appeared in print. The first two chapters originally formed part of the draft for a projected large volume. The fourth chapter, on some aspects of medieval philosophy, was written as a talk for an historical society in the University of London, but for certain reasons the meeting of the student society at which the paper was to have been read never took place. The sixth chapter, on the nature of metaphysics, is the text of a talk which was given, if I remember correctly, to the Collingwood Society at Pembroke College, Oxford, in 1964. I dare say that I might express myself rather differently nowadays, but it represents what I thought at the time. The seventh chapter, on Marx and history, is the text of a contribution to a one-day symposium on Marx which took place at the University of Santa Clara in California during the academic year 1977-78. The symposium was intended for a general audience, not only students but also other persons who might be interested, and contributors were asked to bear this in mind both in their choice of subject and in their treatment of it. The last essay, on Peter Wust, was written a considerable time ago as a tribute to a German philosopher whom I knew personally and for whom I had both respect and affection. Wust is not a well-known thinker, but the essay may perhaps be of some interest as a brief sketch of the life and thought of a professor at the University of Münster in Westphalia, whose tenure of the chair of philosophy (1930-40) coincided for seven years with the Nazi régime but whose thought was strongly opposed to the ideology of the then rulers of Germany.

The third chapter of this book is the text of a talk given at the 1977 convention of the American Catholic Philosophical Association at Detroit. It was subsequently printed in the *Proceedings of the American Catholic Philosophical Association*, Volume LI (pp. 75-86), edited by George F. McLean, OMI. I express my thanks to the editor and the Association for their kind permission to reprint the text here.

The fifth chapter, reflections on analytic philosophy, is a talk which I gave at the third international symposium of the

Hellenic Society for Humanistic Studies, which was held at Athens and Pelion in 1975. It was subsequently printed in the *Proceedings of the Third International Humanistic Symposium at Athens and Pelion* (Athens, 1977, pp. 249-64). I acknowledge with thanks the kind permission given me by Professor Aristoxenos Skiadas, President of the Hellenic Society for Humanistic Studies, to reprint the text here. The talk was intended for an audience which I expected to be somewhat unfavourably disposed to any line of philosophical thought which pays serious attention to 'ordinary language'. From the discussion following the talk I concluded that my expectations were fulfilled in at any rate some cases. No sensible person believes that ordinary language is the final criterion of truth. But in certain areas there are good reasons for taking it as a point of departure, as a 'first word', to borrow a phrase from J.L. Austin. Some people seem to think however that philosophizing starts when common sense has been left behind.

CHAPTER 1

ON THE HISTORY OF PHILOSOPHY

*A terminological point – the subject-matter of history
of philosophy – approaches to the subject: doxographical, through individuals and through problems, psychological – philosophy and other cultural factors – the
presuppositions of philosophers – division into periods
– history of philosophy and critical discussion.*

1. Taken by itself, in abstraction from context, the term 'history of philosophy' is ambiguous. On the one hand it may refer
to the actual historical development of philosophical thought,
in the Greco-Roman world, for example, or in India. On the
other hand it can be used, and, I suppose, generally is used, to
refer to written accounts of such developments. Thus one might
say of a book, 'this is an account of the history of Greek philosophy'. The possible ambiguity might be avoided by reserving
the term 'history of philosophy' for the actual historical development of philosophical thought and by employing some such
phrase as 'historiography of philosophy' to refer to written
accounts of this development. But this cumbersome procedure
is unnecessary. The sense in which 'history of philosophy' is
being used is generally clear enough from the context.

In making a distinction between the actual historical development of philosophical thought and historians' reconstructions
of it, I am obviously assuming a common-sense point of view.
The assumption might perhaps be challenged on the ground that
the past exists only in our reconstructions of it, and that there is
nothing with which we can compare the reconstructions. In
other words, there is only history in the sense of historiography.
This line of objection however is connected with the problem of
objectivity, which will be considered in the next chapter. Mean-
while I propose simply to assume what I believe to be the case,
namely that we can sensibly make a distinction between history
of philosophy in the sense of historiography and history of
philosophy in the sense of that which is reconstructed or re-
counted, with varying degrees of success of course, in written
histories of philosophy.

3

2. If it is asked what histories of philosophy are about, the obvious answer is that they are concerned with the historical development of philosophical thought, in a given period or area or whatever. This is the historian's subject-matter. But what is to count as philosophical thought? Should we, for example, appeal to common linguistic usage or practice, claiming that the historian ought to treat as philosophy all that is commonly regarded as falling under this label and excluding all that is not so labelled? Or does the historian need to formulate or endorse some definition of philosophy, which he then applies to delimit his subject-matter?

Objections can be raised against both these policies. Against the first it can be argued that there is no one constant and uniform linguistic practice, but that ideas of the nature and scope of philosophy have undergone change, and that even today there are somewhat different concepts of philosophy. To be sure, nobody would describe philately as philosophy; and, as far as I am aware, it never has been so described. Mathematics however was once regarded as a branch of philosophy, whereas nowadays it is not so regarded. Does the appeal to linguistic practice mean that the historian should be guided simply by existing practice? This may seem to be a sensible claim; but is it not part of the historian's job to exhibit past concepts of philosophy, to note the changes which have taken place, and to explain why they have occurred?

Against the second policy mentioned above it can be argued that every definition of philosophy is formulated from within philosophy, that it expresses a personal position, and that the effect of some definitions at any rate would be unduly restrictive, in the selection of subject-matter that is to say. Suppose, for example, that an historian were to formulate a definition of philosophy in the light of neopositivist convictions, and that he then used this definition to delimit his subject-matter. Presumably this would result in the exclusion of metaphysics, at any rate of the type represented by Plotinus in the West and by the Vedānta philosophers in India. And this procedure would hardly be what we normally expect of the historian. Moreover, it could be reasonably argued that it would be a case not only of what is normally expected but also of what is legitimately expected. For the historian should pay attention to the sort of philosophy which, in the relevant period, has been regarded as important and significant. The historian might indeed adopt a wide description of philosophy such as that suggested on one occasion by Bertrand Russell, namely the no man's land between science on the one hand and theology on the other. But even this rather vague description is open to objection, if taken as a guide for the historian of philosophy in delimiting his material. For example, lines of inquiry which are now regarded as belonging to science were once classified as pertaining to philosophy. Again, how are we to understand the term 'theology'? We could hardly ascribe to theology, as distinct from philosophy, all talk about God or the Absolute. Aquinas, for example, distinguished between 'the theology which belongs to sacred doctrine' and 'that theology which is a part of philosophy'.[1] And Hegel regarded philosophy as concerned with the nature and self-development of the Absolute or, as he liked to say on occasion, of God. Would it be reasonable for the historian to exclude consideration of all metaphysics of God or of the Absolute, on the ground that it belonged to theology? We could indeed interpret 'theology' in the sense of what Aquinas called 'sacred doctrine', namely as reasoning which employs premises which are believed to have been revealed by God and the truth of which rests on divine authority.[2] Though however we could perfectly well use Aquinas's distinction in order to mark off systematic Christian theology from metaphysics as part of philosophy,[3] difficulties arise if this sort of distinction is employed in a more general way and without Aquinas's presuppositions about the unique character of the Bible as the expression of divine revelation. For example, in the Vedic schools of India allowance was made for the authority of the sacred texts, the Vedas, and the thinkers of these schools often referred to these texts. If therefore an historian of Indian philosophy were to adopt Russell's obviously light-hearted description of philosophy as the no man's land between science and theology and then used it in the delimitation of his subject-matter, he could make out at any rate a plausible case for omitting a very large part of what is usually regarded as Indian philosophy. But this would hardly be a policy likely to satisfy the historian's readers.

There are of course other questions which can be raised in regard to delimitation of the subject-matter of the historian of philosophy. For example, when writing about philosophy in

China Professor Fung Yu-Lan argued that a distinction should be made between philosophy and religion.[4] For instance, Buddhist philosophical thought should be carefully distinguished from Buddhism as religion, and Taoist philosophy from Taoism as a religion. Yu-Lan's point is, I think, a sensible one, and in a general sort of way his stipulation can be complied with fairly easily. No great difficulty is involved in, for instance, distinguishing between Buddhist philosophical thought and the popular religious practices of, say, Pure Land Buddhism, or between the philosophical thought of the Hindu schools on the one hand and popular Hindu religion on the other. At times however philosophy has obviously been religiously oriented. The thought of Plotinus is an example. And most of the traditional Indian philosophy has been geared to enlightenment and liberation. If therefore Yu-Lan's stipulation were accepted, and if it were understood as implying that religiously-oriented thought was not really philosophy, a great deal of Indian thought would have to be omitted from histories of Indian philosophy.[5] It would however be absurd to omit from what purported to be a history of Indian philosophy any treatment of Śamkhara Rāmānuja, Madhva and other philosophers whose thought can be described as having a religious orientation. In other words, it is difficult to define religion, as anyone knows who has tried to do so.

It may be said that the concept of argumentation is relevant to the distinction between philosophy and religion. If, for example, a doctrine is presented as the conclusion of a process of reasoning and not simply as an expression of faith, it can count as philosophical, provided of course that it would not be more appropriately described as a scientific hypothesis. The fact that the doctrine might be described as 'religious' would be irrelevant, provided that it was presented as a conclusion of philosophical argument. In other words, we can perfectly well distinguish between religiously oriented philosophy which is none the less philosophy and religious beliefs which are the expression of faith, resting not on philosophical reasoning, but on what is, or is deemed to be, divine revelation or an inspired sacred text.

This seems to be true as far as it goes. But we are not yet out of the wood. For example, if one reads an account of the development of Japanese thought prior to the Meiji restoration of 1868 and the opening to the West, one may well be left wondering whether one has been reading a history of philosophy in Japan or a list of the tenets of a large number of Buddhist sects. Again, in the work referred to above Fung Yu-Lan drew attention to the fact that early Chinese philosophy was not only largely aphoristic and illustrative in character but also tended to be suggestive, like Chinese poetry and painting, in the sense that meaning was suggested rather than stated precisely, with the consequence that it was open to a great variety of interpretations, each of which could claim to be correct. The question arises therefore whether this sort of thing is to be counted as philosophy and included in a history of philosophy.

It is difficult, if not impossible, to state criteria which will enable us to answer all the questions mentioned above in a definitive manner. For example, at what point the historian of philosophy in a certain area or nation or culture should begin is a question which,within limits, must be left to his personal judgment in regard to relevance.To explain both the origins and certain features of what would generally be recognized as the early philosophy of a given culture an historian may judge it appropriate to include reference to myths which would not normally be classified under the heading of philosophy. But common sense places limits to this procedure. It would obviously be inappropriate to include a detailed treatment of Greek mythology in a work on Greek philosophy, even if some references to mythology are relevant in treating, for instance, of some pre-Socratic philosophers.

In the present writer's opinion common sense will carry us a good distance in answering some of the questions which I have raised. Common sense suggests, for example, that an historian of Greek philosophy should include an account of Greek metaphysical speculation, even if he personally has little use for metaphysics, but that it would be odd and inappropriate if he were to include a detailed account of the development of Greek mathematics. This suggestion may seem to involve an inconsistency. On the one hand mathematics was once counted as part of philosophy. For Aristotle it was a branch of theoretical philosophy. It is no longer classified as part of philosophy. Hence in suggesting that it would be inappropriate for the historian of Greek philosophy to include a detailed account of the development of mathematics in ancient Greece it may seem that I am taking our present-day concept of philosophy as a criterion. On the other hand there have been, and doubtless still are, philosophers in the modern world who think that metaphysics belong to a past stage of human thought. If therefore I insist that the historian of Greek philosophy should include an account of metaphysical speculation, including that of Plotinus, it may seem that this insistence is based on the contention that the historian should respect the ideas of philosophy current at the time at which he is writing. I may thus appear to be operating with two conflicting criteria. I do not think however that there is really any objectionable inconsistency. On the one hand the separation of mathematics from philosophy has not involved the demise of mathematics. It is a flourishing subject, taught in departments of mathematics; and accounts of its historical development are written by others than historians of philosophy. Obviously, the historian of Greek philosophy can be expected to mention the wide meaning then given to the word 'philosophy'; and he can also be expected to explain ideas which can be considered as belonging to the philosophy of mathematics, such as Aristotle's account of mathematical 'objects'.[6] For the rest, he will refer to mathematics itself only in so far as he judges it to be relevant to what we would call philosophy, as in the case of Plato. A systematic account of the development of mathematics in ancient Greece would reasonably be considered superfluous. On the other hand metaphysics has not become, and could not become, an autonomous discipline separate from philosophy. It is either philosophy or nothing. Hence the historian of the philosophy of a period in which metaphysical speculation was a prominent feature cannot justifiably pass it over on the ground that he himself believes that it has little, if any, cognitive value.[7] He is obviously entitled to express his own view in critical discussion, if he wishes to do so. But he ought not to let his personal idea of what philosophy ought to be distort or limit his picture of what it has been. All this seems to me a matter of common sense.

In regard to the relation between philosophy and religion, the fact that a given system of thought can be described as having a religious orientation does not disqualify it from classification as philosophy. Consider classical Indian philosophy. As has already been noted, most of the Indian systems were oriented to enlightenment and liberation, often to the realization of oneness with the Absolute or, in the more theistic line of thought, with God. But this does not alter the fact that there was a great deal of sophisticated argumentation in Indian philosophy. Logic was highly developed, and the schools supported their various positions by argument. Recognition of the authority of the Vedas by the Vedic schools can be misleading. There was no ecclesiastical authority qualified to pronounce on the orthodoxy or unorthodoxy of interpretations of the sacred texts; and in practice philosophers read back into the texts, or emphasized those passages which seemed best to support, the views which they believed to be most consonant with reason and experience. It would be absurd to refuse the title of philosopher to Sánkhara, for example, on the ground that his thought was geared to realization of man's relation to the One. If we adopted this policy, we should apply it to Spinoza too.[8] It is true that Śamkhara represented his system as based on the Upanishads, whereas Spinoza did not claim the authority of the Bible for his account of the universe.[9] At the same time Śamkhara's Advaita Vedānta was supported by arguments of a philosophical character.

Except for those who hesitate to describe as 'philosophical' any system of thought which is oriented to a religious end, Indian philosophy does not really create much difficulty. For the logical structure of the arguments employed is discernible, whether we accept the arguments or not. Much more difficulty is caused by, say, Japanese thought prior to the introduction of western philosophy. For one can easily get the impression that one is faced by a series of assertions which express Confucian or Buddhist teaching introduced from China, and that these assertions are not supported by any recognizable sustained argument. The Indians had their logic, that of the Nyāya school and that of the Buddhist logicians. But though Buddhist logic was introduced into Japan by way of China, it seems to have been kept as a preserve of Buddhist monks, used in the exegesis of sacred texts. It was not disseminated, and logical studies were not developed. Some of the assertions made by Japanese thinkers and religious figures might indeed count as philosophical assertions; but the point is that the process of philosophizing, if by this is meant logically structured reasoning or argument, is far from being a conspicuous feature. A westerner may thus conclude that there was little, if any, philosophizing in Japan;

and he may feel that any accusation of western prejudice is unfounded, inasmuch as what he is looking for is not a replica of western philosophy but simply evidence of logical structure and sustained argument, such as we find in the classical Indian systems.

Japan's dependence on China, in regard to both Confucianism and Buddhism, obviously does not entail the conclusion that there was no philosophical thought in Japan before 1868. It has been maintained that Confucian ethics and social philosophy and Buddhist thought underwent adaptation to Japanese ways of thinking. Further, it may be the case, as I have heard suggested, that thought-patterns can be found which exemplify what can reasonably be described as philosophical reflection, even if they seem strange to the western mind. Again, I have heard it argued that though the thirteenth-century thinker Dōgen introduced into Japan the Soto sect of Zen Buddhism and exhorted his disciples to abandon all literature save the Buddhist sacred texts and the writings of the Zen masters, he can legitimately be described as a phenomenologist who concerned himself, in a Zen context, with pre-reflective experience.

However this may be, it seems reasonable to claim that in trying to delimit the subject-matter of the history of philosophy we should allow for the possibility of there being different styles of philosophizing, related to rather different ways of thought characteristic of different peoples or cultures.[10] At the same time, if we can legitimately group together different ways of thinking under the common heading of philosophy or philosophizing, there must be something in common. It is not a question of arguing that there must be something in common because we use the same word or label. It is a question of whether there is sufficient ground for using the same word. To be sure, it is hardly to be expected that general agreement can easily be reached in regard to the application of this criterion. For example, historians of Islamic philosophy are accustomed to include treatments of Sufi thought, though some philosophers, I suppose, would prefer to relegate it to an account of the religion of Islam. Again, reference has been made above to possible differences of opinion about the propriety of describing Buddhist thought in pre-1868 Japan as philosophy. To come nearer home, though historians of Greek philosophy have been accustomed to include a treatment of the pre-Socratics (rightly, in my opinion), some philosophers prefer to regard most of the pre-Socratics as primitive scientists and believe that Greek philosophy really started with Socrates. Though however differences of opinion on such matters may well continue to exist, especially in view of the difficulties which arise in defining such general terms as 'philosophy', 'religion' and 'science', intelligent discussion of the issues is at any rate possible. Moreover, borderline cases apart, there is evidently a substantial measure of agreement as to how the word 'philosophy' should be understood, when it is a question of histories of philosophical thought. Controversy obviously cannot be terminated simply by claiming that for the purposes of the historian of philosophy regard must be paid to what philosophy has been rather than to what anyone, including the historian considered as a philosopher, believes that philosophy ought to be. For we cannot decide what philosophy has been without some idea of the range of meaning of the term.[11] And here there can be some differences of opinion. However, there are, for example, kinds of problems which are generally recognized as philosophical and which have had a transcultural incidence, being found, for instance, in both western and Indian philosophy. Differences of opinion in regard to certain issues does not entail the conclusion that use of the word 'philosophy' can be nothing more than the result of arbitrary decision, and that the historian of philosophy can reasonably include or exclude anything he likes. Decisions, if challenged, should be supportable by reasons. The reasons adduced for a certain decision or choice may not always win universal acceptance. But there is nothing odd or exceptional in this situation. If one thinks that some proffered reasons are bad ones, it does not necessarily follow that there are no good ones.

The foregoing remarks seem to amount to the rather banal statement, that the subject-matter of the historian of philosophy is the historical development of philosophical thought, and that, while there is a measure of substantial agreement about what should count as philosophy for this purpose, there are cases in which different judgments can be supported by arguments which cannot properly be dismissed out of hand. This statement seems to imply that the historian of philosophy should confine his attention to what can reasonably be described as philosophical thought. For this, or the historical development of it, is said to constitute his subject-matter. An objection can however be raised against this implication, the objection, that is to say, that philosophy does not pursue an isolated path of its own, but is influenced by a variety of extra-philosophical factors, and that the historian of philosophy either should or is entitled to include consideration of such influences in his subject-matter.

3. Discussion of this issue can be postponed for the moment. First of all I wish to say something about different approaches to the history of philosophy or, more precisely, different ways of writing the history of philosophy.

(i) When considering different approaches to the historiography of philosophy, it is unnecessary to say much about what is commonly described as the doxographical approach. In works which exemplify this approach the opinions of philosophers are listed and classified in some way or other, probably with some criticism or comment. In the ancient world Theophrastus, who succeeded Aristotle as head of the Peripatetic school and who died about 286 BC, compiled a work in eighteen books *On the Opinions of the Physical Philosophers*, the opinions being classified under topics.[12] A later work, which is still extant, is the celebrated account of the lives and opinions of the Greek philosophers by Diogenes Laërtius.[13] The author is much given to recounting anecdotes and stories, sometimes incompatible stories, about the philosophers, while his method of classification obscures chronological sequence and the logical connections between different philosophies. Though however in stating the opinions of the philosophers, especially the early ones, he evidently relies to a considerable extent on previous secondary sources and sometimes juxtaposes different accounts, his work contains a good deal of valuable information and also some direct quotations or excerpts from primary sources, as in the case of Epicurus.

In the Middle Ages Walter Burleigh, an English Franciscan who died about 1345, composed a similar work *On the Life and Manners of the Philosophers (De vita ac moribus philosophorum)*, which was printed at Cologne in 1472.[14] Mention can also be made of Thomas Stanley's three-volume *History of Philosophy*, which was published at London in 1655-61 and served for a considerable time as a textbook of Greek philosophy.[15] As for Johann Jakob Brucker's *Critical History of Philosophy from the*

Beginning of the World up to Our Time,[16] the title suggests something more than a doxography, in the sense of a list of opinions. In view however of the fact that Brucker's critical treatment tends to take the form of awarding the philosophers good or bad marks in so far as they agree with or depart from his own convictions, his work is generally thought of as belonging to the doxographical tradition, even if the author's learning can be said to mark a transition to a different approach.

The doxographical approach is defective rather than entirely valueless. To ask what a given philosopher held is a natural question; and complaint might justifiably be made about any history of philosophy which did not indicate the conclusions at which philosophers arrived. This hardly needs saying. At the same time simply to list philosophers' opinions or conclusions is not very illuminating. This procedure fails to exhibit the problems confronting a given philosopher, the genesis and nature of those problems, the way in which he dealt with them, the process of reasoning by which he arrived at his conclusions, and so on. In other words, the whole process of philosophizing, philosophy as an activity, is passed over. And we are presented simply with results or conclusions. We can see this sort of thing in a number of old-fashioned textbooks of Scholastic philosophy, in which the opinions of 'adversaries' were mentioned, without any real attempt to explain how they came to form these opinions. For example, the reader might be informed that Kant held that space and time were 'subjective', and that this opinion was patently absurd. Unless therefore the student pursued further study on his own, he would not understand how Kant came to adopt certain positions. Similarly, the student might be informed that according to Berkeley material things were 'ideas' and that they did not exist unperceived, without any real explanation of Berkeley's line of thought.[17] At the same time it is obvious that a reader should be able to learn from a work on the history of philosophy what the philosophers in question held or believed to be true.

As for anecdotes about philosophers and details of their lives and peculiarities, relevance to philosophical thought is obviously a sensible criterion. At the same time fanaticism is to be avoided. If an historian wishes to introduce some light relief by referring to Kant's concern with punctuality, it would be pedantic to object, provided that the exposition of Kant's philosophy does not suffer as the result of an accumulation of amusing anecdotes.

(ii) A purely doxographical approach finds no supporters nowadays. It is therefore unnecessary to waste any more time on it. But it is not at all so obvious whether the best way of writing history of philosophy is in terms of individuals, especially of course the outstanding philosophers, or of movements of thought or of problems. It seems true to say that historians of philosophy generally tend to treat their subject-matter in terms of individuals, in the sense, for example, that the thought of Plato is more or less covered in all its principal aspects before treatment of Aristotle is begun. But there is at any rate one notable history of philosophy, namely Windelband's,[18] in which the historical development of philosophical thought is treated in terms of distinguishable problems rather than in terms of individuals. Given this procedure, a philosopher's thought might be discussed in several chapters. His contribution to the body-mind problem, for example, would be discussed in a continuous treatment of this problem as handled by a number of thinkers over a certain tract of time, while his contribution to ethical problems would be discussed in a similar way elsewhere.

In the opinion of the present writer we cannot say which is the best way, in an absolute sense, of writing history of philosophy, though we can indeed make a judgment about what is relatively best, or at any rate preferable, in relation, that is to say, to a specified aim or in relation to the kind of reader envisaged. It is arguable that for the general reader it is preferable that emphasis should be placed on outstanding individual thinkers, and that the thought of each should be treated as a whole and continuously. For example, Kant's three *Critiques* can be regarded as forming a unity, and their interrelations would tend to be obscured, if, say, Kant's epistemological problems were treated in a chapter or set of chapters in which the author then went on to discuss Fichte and Hegel, while Kant's ethics was treated elsewhere, in conjunction with the ethical theories of other philosophers. At the same time, a treatment of the history of philosophy by problems can be illuminating for readers who are already reasonably well-acquainted with philosophy and its historical development.

Besides, the approaches to the history of philosophy mentioned above are not necessarily mutually exclusive. For example, even if an historian treats the philosophies of Locke, Berkeley and Hume as successive units, this does not prevent him from displaying their respective rôles in a movement of thought, the development of classical British empiricism, and clarifying the relations between them, as well as the particular characteristics of each. Again, successive treatment of the philosophies of the leading German idealists of the nineteenth century is not incompatible with locating each in a general movement of thought. Further, there is room for a variety of arrangements. If it is considered desirable to treat Fichte, Schelling and Hegel successively, in that order, a good case can obviously be made out for confining the treatment of Schelling to those phases of his thought which are relevant to the development of Hegel's thought and reserving Schelling's later thought for subsequent treatment. This is a matter which must be left to the judgment of the historian. One can hardly pass an absolute judgment about which is the best policy to pursue.

There is one point arising out of what has been said above which perhaps calls for brief comment. I have referred to 'outstanding' philosophers; and it might be asked, 'what are the criteria for assessing whether a philosopher is outstanding or not? Or, if we wish to speak of greatness, what are the criteria for identifying great or eminent philosophers?' In practice people doubtless tend to think of those figures as outstanding whom they are accustomed to hear described as such. But the reply 'those philosophers are outstanding who are commonly conceived as outstanding' is not likely to satisfy the inquiring mind.

It seems to me that we can think of several criteria. For example, it is reasonable to consider as outstanding a philosopher who has proved capable of speaking to or stimulating the minds of people living outside his own age, or even outside his own culture. Thus Spinoza can still exercise a powerful attraction on some minds, and Śamkhara has attracted and stimulated people who were not Indians. Perhaps such thinkers retain a power of attraction because they have expressed in an impressive way possible ways of seeing the world and man's place in it. Again, we might well regard as outstanding any philosopher who has exercised a powerful influence on the course of philosophical thought. Such were Kant and Wittgenstein in their different ways. Further, if a philosopher opened up a number of significant questions or problems and clearly raised the standard of philosophizing, as Plato did, he obviously qualifies for an honorific epithet such as 'outstanding' or 'eminent'. And one might think of other criteria too. My point is simply that criteria can be mentioned, and that talk about outstanding philosophers is not simply a concession to linguistic fashion.

It is hardly necessary to explain that it is not my intention to suggest that a history of, say, Greek or medieval philosophy should consist of a series of detached treatments of eminent thinkers. The historian tries to exhibit the historical development of philosophical thought, and it is his business to make clear connections and movements, the rise of new attitudes, methods, problems and so on. It is however obvious that philosophical thought is the thought of people, philosophers. Some of them are original thinkers, while others are epigoni, more bearers of a tradition than creative minds. All that I have been maintaining is that for most readers it is probably preferable, for specifiable reasons, that the philosophies of the more significant thinkers should be treated as unities, rather than that the thought of, say, Spinoza should be broken up and treated piecemeal under different headings, such as the body-mind problem, ethical problems, philosophy of religion, and so on. I do not claim that any one approach is best in an absolute sense. Windelband's approach may well be admirably suited for some purposes.

What I have been saying applies primarily to accounts of western philosophy, including accounts of Jewish and Islamic thought in the Middle Ages. We are accustomed to thinking in terms of individual philsophers such as Plato, Aristotle, Avicenna, Descartes, Spinoza, Hume, and so on. That is to say, the emphasis is generally placed on individual thinkers rather than on sets of doctrines exemplified by individuals. In the case of Indian philosophy however there is a marked tendency to think in terms of schools, Nyàya. Sámkhya, Advaita Vedānta, and so forth. To a certain extent this may be due to the considerable difficulty experienced in determining chronological relations in the area of earlier Indian philosophy. We are perfectly well aware that Aristotle was junior to Plato, that he spent some years in the Platonic Academy, and that he came to criticize a number of Platonic theories. There is no great diffi-

culty therefore in discussing the relations between Aristotle and
Plato. Similarly, we know the dates of Kant and Fichte, and we
know Fichte's reaction to Kant's theory of the thing-in-itself.
When however we cannot be sure whether *A* lived before or
after or at the same time as *B*, we are hardly in a position to
determine the historical relations between them. At the same
time, in regard to classical Indian philosophy it is not simply a
question of difficulty in determining chronological sequences
and relations of influence. In India schools enjoyed a much
greater longevity than western schools; and attention was paid
more to the doctrines of the schools than to the individuals who
represented them.[19] To be sure, there are well-known individual
philosophers, such as Samkhara, Rāmānuja and Madhva and, in
Buddhist thought, Nāgārjuna. But it seems true to say that
much more emphasis was laid on ideas, presented as faithful
developments of the doctrines of sacred texts, than on individuals. It is natural therefore that in accounts of the historical
development of classical Indian philosophy the subject-matter
should be approached in terms of schools rather than in terms of
individuals. The existence and continuance of the schools are
historical facts, and they obviously have to be given prominence by any historian of philosophy in India. The traditions
of the schools have however been carried on and developed by
individual thinkers, and any increase in relevant historical knowledge would doubtless result in greater prominence being given
to individual contributions.[20]

(iii) Reference to philosophical thought as being the thought
of individuals brings us on to the subject of the psychological
approach to the history of philosophy, the extreme expression
of which would be explanation of a philosopher's thought in
terms of his character, personality, life or ideals or even of infra-
conscious factors. It is obvious that in many cases we lack
sufficient knowledge even to make out a plausible case in support of a psychological interpretation of a given thinker's philosophy, whereas in certain instances, such as those of Kierkegaard
and Nietzsche, we have sufficient evidence to hazard psychological explanations, if we wish to do so. However, I am concerned here not so much with the availability of evidence to support such explanations as with the question whether a psychological approach is an appropriate way of writing history of philosophy.

As a preliminary remark, one can say that there are two conflicting positions in regard to this matter. But care has to be
exercised in locating the point of conflict. The positions could
be stated in such a way that they would be compatible. They
can also be stated in such a way that they are clearly opposed.

The first position which I have in mind is the thesis that as all
philosophical reflection is pursued by human beings, creatures
of flesh and blood with characters and temperaments of their
own, we cannot properly understand the philosophizing of any
thinker, unless it is seen and interpreted in the light of the
thinker's personality or psychological make-up and basic moti-
vation, so far as we are able to know it. To illustrate this point
of view we can refer to Miguel de Unamuno's statement that 'in
most of the histories which I know, philosophical systems are
presented to us as if they had grown out of one another spontaneously, and their authors, the philosophers, appear as mere
pretexts. The inner biography of the philosophers, of the man
who philosophized, is given a secondary place. And yet it is
precisely this inner biography which explains for us most
things'.[21] The meaning of the term 'inner biography' is not
quite clear. But after making these general remarks Unamuno
gives an example which helps to show the sort of thing of which
he is thinking. He refers to the transition from Kant's first
Critique to the second, and he interprets it as showing that Kant
reconstructed with his heart what he had overthrown or demol-
ished with his head. According to the Spanish philosopher, Kant
as a man was not resigned to the thought of extinction at death
and therefore took the leap of what he described as practical or
moral faith.

There are various objections which might be brought against
what Unamuno says. For example, though it is open to anyone
to argue that in the first *Critique* Kant did in fact demolish the
beliefs which he tried to reinstate by way of the moral consciousness, Kant himself believed that in his first *Critique* he
had simply shown that freedom, immortality and the existence
of God could not be theoretically proved, not that they could
be disproved or shown to be meaningless. Again, Unamuno
passes over the fact that in the second *Critique* Kant gives some
sort of argument for immortality, the merits or demerits of
which can be assessed without bringing in psychological considerations. Presumably however Unamuno is well aware of all

this. A man who passionately desired immortality, even if he believed that it could not be proved, Unamuno ascribes a similar desire or concern to Kant. And he regards this as the significant factor. Kant's argument to support belief in immortality or to show that the belief is not irrational, Unamuno regards as an example of wishful thinking. In his view therefore Kant's postulation of immortality in the second *Critique* is to be explained in terms of Kant's existential concern. It is not a question of denying that Kant's argument can be considered by itself. Rather is it a question of claiming that for an understanding of Kant we have to penetrate deeper than the surface argumentation. Unamuno is accusing historians of philosophy of superficiality rather than denying that arguments can be examined precisely as arguments. To put the matter in another way, the 'explanation' which he has in mind is explanation in terms of 'inner biography', of why a philosopher said what he did, why he pursued a certain line of thought or produced certain arguments, perhaps flimsy ones.

The second point of view alluded to above is that the psychological approach is irrelevant, as far as philosophers and historians of philosophy are concerned. Psychologists are obviously entitled to take philosophers as subjects for psychological analysis, if they wish to do so. But once philosophical ideas have been expressed, they can and should be judged in terms of truth or falsity, without reference to the personal characteristics of the philosophers who conceived them. For example, in a certain book[22] Ludwig Wittgenstein is represented as having had, in his early days in Vienna, passing sexual encounters with young men. Other writers have rejected the charge as lacking a sufficient basis in empirical evidence. The present writer knows nothing about the facts of the case. For the sake of argument however let us suppose that Wittgenstein was at any rate homosexually oriented, as indeed Bertrand Russell believed that he was.[23] Would this fact, if it was a fact, have any bearing on the truth or falsity of, say, the theory of the proposition advanced in the *Tractatus Logico-Philosophicus*? The answer is obviously 'no'.

The reason why I said above that the two positions could be stated in such a way that they would be compatible should be clear enough. Let us assume, for the sake of argument, that Unamuno was right in claiming that Kant could not resign himself to the thought of extinction. This may explain why Kant concerned himself with the subject in the second *Critique*. It is however still open to anyone to admit this and yet to insist that, from the strictly philosophical point of view, we should concentrate on the merits or demerits of Kant's argument to show that belief in immortality is in some sense (a sense which it is difficult to define) an implication of the moral consciousness. Similarly, for the sake of argument let us assume that Wittgenstein was tormented by homosexual inclinations and that he wished to escape from them.[24] This might conceivably help to explain why he took refuge, so to speak, in a rather abstract logical sphere. We could however perfectly well accept this hypothesis and still insist that the question of the adequacy of the picture-theory of the proposition in the *Tractatus* had to be settled in terms of criteria which had nothing to do with the philosopher's sexual inclinations. The two theses would be quite compatible. To confirm this statement, we can take an example from a non-philosophical area. The poetry of Rimbaud and Verlaine should obviously be judged according to the appropriate aesthetic criteria, whatever they may be, without any reference to the sexual goings-on of the two poets. But this does not prevent us from admitting that their sexual relations are relevant to understanding how Rimbaud came to write certain poems.

In the present context however we are concerned not so much with the logical compatibility or incompatibility of the two positions as with the question whether a psychological approach is appropriate to the history of philosophy. In regard to this question I can only state my personal opinion. It is hardly possible to give a demonstrative proof of any particular answer, unless we choose to define history of philosophy in such a way that a certain answer follows by strict logical entailment.

As a general statement, I think that psychological analysis of individual philosophers and history of philosophy, in the sense of an account of the historical development of philosophical thought, an account of the activity of philosophizing through the centuries or over a certain period or in a certain area, should be kept separate. That is to say, while psychologists are perfectly entitled to inquire into the psychological make-up of this or that philosopher, if they wish to do so, and to relate their findings to the philosopher's thought, I do not think that the historian of philosophy should try to play the part of a psychoanalyst. It is not simply a question of the historian probably being an amateur in this field and of his psychological hypotheses being even more speculative than those of the professional psychologist. Rather is it a question of its being the historian's job to give a continuous intelligible and coherent account of the activity of philosophizing, and, if he pursues critical discussion, to evaluate arguments and theories according to logical and philosophical criteria. If he indulges in psychoanalysis of one kind or another, he is likely to obscure the philosophical connections between systems and to give the impression that the validity or invalidity of arguments and the truth or falsity of philosophical statements can be determined by psychological criteria. Readers can easily get the impression that everything has been 'explained', when the philosophical thought has been related to the psychology of the thinker, without any serious attention being paid to the question whether a given argument is sound or not. To take a very simple example, St Thomas Aquinas obviously did not believe in God as a result of his Five Ways. Belief preceded, the proofs came later. It is therefore tempting to dismiss the arguments as expressions of wishful thinking. But in a serious philosophical work this sort of procedure is quite inappropriate. Whether the arguments are in fact sound or not, they have to be judged by logical criteria, not by a summary reference to Aquinas's desires, hidden or otherwise. In fine, the psychological approach to the history of philosophy is not conducive to philosophical education.

Though however the historian of philosophy should avoid giving the impression that the truth or falsity of philosophical statements and the validity or invalidity of arguments can be determined by reference to the psychology of philosophers, it can hardly be denied, I think, that in some cases at any rate light can be shed on the significance of philosophical ideas and theories by seeing them in the light of biographical material and even of what Unamuno called 'inner biography'. Consider, for example, Kierkegaard's theory of stages on life's way, the aesthetic, ethical and religious states. It is certainly arguable that in fixing on these precise stages Kierkegaard was influenced by a series of experiences in his own life. And some knowledge of his life seems to be relevant to our understanding of his thought, in a way in which the fact that Hegel had an illegitimate son does not seem to be relevant to an understanding of absolute idealism. To be sure, the theory of stages on life's way and the phenomenological analyses which Kierkegaard gives of them can be considered in isolation, without, that is to say, reference to Kierkegaard's life. But if we understand the element of universalization of personal experience in the theory as presented by Kierkegaard, we may be less likely to regard the theory as presented as something to be taken or left. We may have a greater flexibility in our approach. If so, some knowledge of his life is philosophically relevant. How much, if any, biographical material an historian of philosophy includes must be left to his personal judgments. Practical considerations have a part to play. All that I am claiming is that biographical material and 'inner biography' can be relevant to an understanding of philosophical theories. There are, I think, aspects of Nietzsche's thought which can be better understood in the light of his intentions. If, for example, it is pretty clear that he intended the theory of the Eternal Recurrence primarily as a test of strength, rather than as an empirical hypothesis or a metaphysical truth, we shall treat it in the appropriate way and not by asking whether it can be shown to be true or false, when truth and falsity are understood rather differently from the way in which Nietzsche understood them.[25]

It can be objected that even if what I have been saying is true, it by no means follows that the historian of philosophy should introduce 'inner biography', or even outer biography, into his work. For it is arguable that writers such as Kierkegaard and Nietzsche ought not to be described as philosophers. If labels are required, some other way of classifying them should be found. In any case, philosophical ideas, once expressed, are what they are and should be treated as public property, so to speak, without reference to the life or psychology of the thinker. To evaluate the theory of the proposition in the *Tractatus* it is not necessary to know anything about Wittgenstein. To evaluate the arguments in Spinoza's *Ethics*, we do not require any reference to Spinoza's life or personality. And if there are thinkers whose thought cannot properly be understood without its being related to their lives, intentions or psychology, this is a very good reason for not describing these thinkers as philosophers.

This line of objection illustrates the point which I made above, namely that we cannot give a definitive answer to the question whether a psychological approach has or has not any place in the history of philosophy, unless we so define philosophy that writers such as Kierkegaard and Nietzsche are excluded. But it is also possible to understand philosophy in a wider sense. Kierkegaard certainly attacked 'philosophy' (that is, the Hegelian system); but this does not necessarily mean that he was not a philosopher. For he might attack 'philosophy' for philosophical reasons, among others at any rate. As for Nietzsche, we can reasonably allow for his own idea of the function of philosophy, even if it is not ours. In general, a history of philosophy which passed over in complete silence thinkers such as Pascal, Kierkegaard and Nietzsche, might reasonably be considered inadequate. True, it would be possible to expound their ideas and the arguments to support them (when arguments were forthcoming) without reference to biographical material or to 'inner biography'. My sole claim however is that such reference can in some cases be relevant to understanding. I still stand of course by the judgment that in the case of propositions which can be properly described as true or false, they should be examined in terms of the appropriate criteria, and that the historian of philosophy should be careful not to give the impression that an understanding of how a philosopher came to assert p is not equivalent to an understanding of the truth or falsity of p.

A final point. In discussing the psychological approach to the history of philosophy I have been referring to the activity of explaining the thought of an individual philosopher in psychological terms. This approach is obviously most likely to be found in monographs on those philosophers of whom, as men, we know a good deal and whose characters make a psychological treatment of their thought seem plausible. It is also possible however to speculate about the psychological grounds of recurrent tendencies.[26] For example, it has been suggested that there is in some people a psychological predisposition to monism, and that it is largely for this reason that monism tends to recur in the historical development of philosophical thought. In theory at least this sort of idea is more likely to be employed in general histories of philosophy.[27] For if we think that we have grounds for diagnosing a psychological predisposition to, say, monism in the case of monists of whose personality and temperament we know a good deal, we may be inclined to postulate a similar predisposition to monism in monist philosophers of whom, as individual human beings, we know very little. In other words, we would be relating X's thought not so much to X's pecular characteristics as to a psychological predisposition which could occur also in Y and Z.

Suggestions of this kind seem to me largely conjectural. But I am obviously not in a position to deny that there are psychological predispositions to certain lines of thought. In fact, I am inclined to think that there probably are, though it by no means follows that they are irresistible. I might, for instance, be predisposed to monism, yet none the less reject it on, say, common-sense or experiential grounds. In any case it seems to me that the historian of philosophy should concern himself with the ostensible reasons why A or B expounds a monistic theory and with the arguments which he advances in support of it, not with conjectures about possible infra-conscious or pre-reflective psychological factors. Speculation of this sort is best left to psychologists. However, in meta-history, in reflections based on a comparative survey of the histories of philosophy in different cultures, consideration of psychological hypotheses could hardly be excluded, in the sense of being declared illegitimate or inappropriate. If, for example, a philosopher of the history of philosophy, when considering the incidence of monism in East and West, wished to mention and discuss the possibility of psychological factors being involved, I see no compelling reason why he should not do so. My only claim is that the ordinary historian of philosophical thought would be well advised to avoid indulging in any psychological speculation and to lay emphasis instead on properly philosophical discussion.

4. The impression may have been given that I envisage the historian of philosophy as attending exclusively to the logical connections between philosophies, to the contents of these philosophies, the ideas and theories advanced in them and the arguments adduced to support them, and to the influence of one philosopher on another. The objection can then be raised that philosophy does not pursue an isolated path of its own but is related in many ways to man's other activities and to other cultural factors. Is it not the historian's business to set

any philosophy in its historical and cultural context and to exhibit its interrelations with other cultural disciplines and with the structure, features and problems of its contemporary society? If this is not done, a false impression is surely given of the historical development of philosophical thought, irrespective of whether the historian is treating of philosophy over a long period of time or of a selected movement or phase of philosophical thought, of the philosophy of a whole culture or of a part or parts of it.

Nobody in his senses would deny that philosophy has been affected in a variety of ways by extra-philosophical factors. For the truth of the statement is evident. To take an obvious example, in the Middle Ages not only was theology regarded as the chief science but also most of the well-known philosophers were primarily theologians. It is natural therefore that theology should have influenced philosophy in specifiable ways, by suggesting certain problems, for instance. Indeed, medieval philosophical thought cannot be adequately understood without reference to the status and influence of theology in the relevant period.[28] Again, while mathematics has at times influenced philosophy, by suggesting, for example, a model method, in the post-medieval world the development of the empirical sciences has exercised a very considerable influence on philsophical thought, sometimes in regard to problematics, sometimes on the level of theory (as in the case of the evolutionary hypothesis), sometimes by suggesting a paradigm of method.[29] Further, if we turn to social and political philosophy, it is clear enough that it has been profoundly influenced by the contemporary socio-political background or situation. Plato's political theory is an obvious case in point. So is the philosophy of Karl Marx. Again, conflicts in contemporary culture and society can find their reflection or expression in the philosophical field. We can think, for example, of the tension between the scientific and religious mentalities[30] and, on the social-political level, of the conflicts between the interests of institutions and groups. Thus in the Middle Ages tensions between Church and State were reflected in political philosophy, while with Marx we find a reflection of the conflict between the interests of different classes.

It does not follow that philosophy is simply an ineffective reflection of the influence of extra-philosophical factors of one kind or another. Philosophical ideas can certainly exercise an influence, through, that is to say, the activities of the people who accept them. This is obvious in the case of Marxism. Again, while it would be absurd to ascribe the French revolution to the influence of the French philosophers of the eighteenth century, we can reasonably claim that the writings of *les philosophes* contributed to forming a mental climate or atmosphere favourable to change. The thinkers of the French Enlightenment were influenced by those features of the contemporary situation which rendered some sort of revolution inevitable, unless the régime was prepared to initiate major changes; but their ideas in turn exercised some influence on the course of events, even if the degree of influence can be exaggerated.[31] One could also refer to the influence of philosophical ideas in, say, China. In fine, the traffic, so to speak, does not proceed simply in one direction. It is a case of the interrelations between philosophy and extra-philosophical factors, of two-way influences.

Before going any further, we should draw attention to the following point. Given the influence on philosophy of extra-philosophical factors, it is possible to push this line of thought to the point at which the philosopher is depicted as being the spokesman of the society in which he belongs, in the sense that his problems and theories are regarded as relevant simply to his time and as having no relevance in a different cultural and social context. It is even possible to use selected historical data as a point of departure for stating a relativist theory of truth. Here however I am concerned simply with the question, to what extent, if any, should the historian of philosophy concern himself with trying to exhibit the interrelations between philosophy and extra-philosophical factors?

It seems to me that the only rules which can be sensibly formulated are negative rules, in the sense of rules which state what ought not to be done. If, for example, an historian chooses to concentrate his attention on the internal relations between philosophies, he has the right to do so. At the same time he should not follow this legitimate approach in a way which involves or implies a denial of the obvious fact that philosophical thought is related in a variety of ways to extra-philosophical factors. Again, if an historian chooses to refer to the relations between philosophy and its cultural and social background, he has the right to do so. But he should not over-look the facts that by no means all philosophical ideas are equally dependent on extra-philosophical factors, that philosophy can in turn exercise an influence, and that there can be (in my opinion at least) philosophical propositions which are true whenever enunciated. Nor should he concentrate on the relations between philosophy and extra-cultural factors to such an extent that the historical development of philosophical thought is obscured. For example, there is a connection between the Romantic movement in Germany and German metaphysical idealism of the early decades of the nineteenth century.[32] But though mention and some discussion of this connection would be perfectly legitimate, the topic should not be allowed to obscure the relations between the relevant idealist philosophies.

In other words, there is room for histories of philosophy in which the emphasis is rather differently placed. We have to leave it to the historian to decide how much or how little reference to the influence of extra-philosophical factors is relevant to his purpose and is likely to facilitate understanding, on the part of the sort of reader whom he has in mind. We cannot justifiably claim that no such reference should be made. But it should be relevant, relevant, that is to say, not in some absolute sense but in relation to a specifiable end or to specifiable purposes. This verdict may seem to be no more than an expression of common sense. But, if so, it is none the worse for that. It may be that an ideal history of philosophy would exhibit and discuss all the factors relevant to the development of philosophy. But an ideal history of philosophy, a history to end all histories, is impracticable, probably impossible.[33]

It might perhaps be claimed that the job of the historian of philosophy is to stick to the story of philosophy proper, and that to discuss the relations between philosophy and extra-philosophical factors is to trespass on the territory of the historian of culture or of the history of ideas. But I do not think that we can make rigid divisions of this sort. All we can reasonably stipulate is that the historian of philosophy should introduce only what is relevant to his main task, giving a coherent and intelligible account of the historical development of philosophical thought. What is relevant and what is not relevant is a question which must be left, in the first instance,[34] to the judgment of the historian himself.

The idea may have occurred to the reader that the psychology of the philosophers is an extra-philosophical factor which may, in some cases at least, be relevant to an understanding of a philosopher's thought. It does not seem to me however that I have been guilty of gross inconsistency, in the sense that this section contradicts or is incompatible with the last. For in regard to biographical material and to what Unamuno described as 'inner biography' I did not assert that such topics should never be introduced into a history of philosophy. I simply emphasized relevance and the importance of avoiding giving the impression that the truth or falsity of statements (or the validity of arguments) can be determined by referring to the psychological make-up of the philosophers who made them. It is true that I referred unfavourably to historians who try to play the role of psychologists, indulging in speculations which it is difficult to check.[35] But I would also take an unfavourable view of historians who wove airy speculations about the influence on philosophy of non-psychological extra-philosophical factors, when there was scant evidence, if any, to support them. In point of fact there are many pretty obvious cases of such influence. And there can be, on occasion, pretty obvious cases of the influence of a philosopher's life and experience on his thought. When this is so, I see no good reason why the historian should be prohibited from referring to the matter, if he wishes to do so. Whether 'personal thinkers'[36] should be accounted philosophers is another question, to which I have already made a brief reference in the last section.

5. As far as western philosophy is concerned, it is customary to divide it into a number of periods, such as ancient, medieval, renaissance and modern philosophy. And there can of course be sub-divisions. Though however this sort of division is usually taken for granted, objections have been raised against it. For example, it has been argued that if we think of the Renaissance in terms of a literary revival, we are quite justified in pushing back its beginning not only to Petrarch (1304-74) and Boccaccio (1313-75) but also to Dante (1265-1321). If we think in terms of an increased knowledge of and interest in Greco-Roman literature, we might well go back to the schools of translators in the later decades of the twelfth century and the early decades

of the thirteenth century. If we think of the Renaissance in terms of the scientific phase, which succeeded the humanistic and literary phase, we ought not to pass over the scientific work of, say, Roger Bacon (c. 1212 – after 1292) and Nicholas Oresme (d. 1382). True, there was, so to speak, a hiatus. Embryonic medieval science did not bear immediate fruit. But it was there none the less. In other words, no definitive lines can be drawn between periods. This is only to be expected as, despite revolutions, history is continuous. There would not even be a revolution unless the grounds for it had been prepared; and features of an old society can persist in a new one. In the sphere of history of philosophy it is all very well to speak of Descartes as the father of modern philosophy; but nobody would now deny that he used a number of traditional concepts and was more influenced by the past than is allowed for by the idea of him as the first of the moderns.

Argument and counter-argument can be prolonged. Thus it might be pointed out on the one hand that though Dante was a master of the Italian language and the greatest Italian poet, he had a medieval outlook, and his thought cannot be properly understood without some knowledge of medieval theology and philosophy. On the other hand it can be pointed out that Petrarch promoted the revival of the classical, especially the Ciceronian style, and that through his vernacular sonnets he promoted the growth of humanistic individualism. On the one hand it can be pointed out, as already mentioned, that Descartes utilized traditional concepts, while on the other side it can be urged that he gave them a new meaning. On the one hand it can be argued that Nicholas of Cusa (1401-64), whose life overlapped with that of Marsilius Ficinus (1433-99), should certainly be counted as a renaissance figure. On the other hand it can be argued that there are elements in his thought which provide justification for assigning him to the medieval period, and that if chronological considerations forbid this move, this is an additional reason for abandoning the division of periods into periods.

It seems to me quite unnecessary to make a song and dance about the matter. It is doubtless salutary if from time to time criticism is directed against our traditional divisions. For such criticism reminds us of continuity and overlapping and of the element of decision or choice in determining the limits of

periods, a decision which is not immune from questioning. In
general, such criticism helps to protect us from the tyranny of
habit, of taking it for granted that our particular way of divid-
ing the material is sacrosanct. It makes us more ready to consider other possible conceptual frameworks. At the same time I
do not think that it is either practicable or desirable to abandon
any sort of division whatsoever, any sort of label. For there are
specifiable differences which give rise to such divisions. For
example, there are specifiable differences between social structures in ancient Greece and the feudal society of the Middle
Ages, just as there are specifiable differences between medieval
society and the industrial society of later times. Again, there are
specifiable differences between the mental outlook which
regards theology as the chief science and the mental outlook for
which the natural sciences constitute the paradigm of scientific
knowledge. It must be remembered however that we can fix our
attention on different characteristics or sets of characteristics.
For example, if the historian of medieval philosophy chooses to
emphasize different social structures as the principal differentiating characteristic, he will not include any treatment of thought
in the Roman empire, the social structures of which differed
from those of the Middle Ages. If however he fixes his attention on the development of thought in the context of Christian
faith, he cannot omit consideration of Christian thought before
the fall of the Roman empire. After all, St Augustine, for example, exercised an influence throughout the whole of the
Middle Ages. Some divisions seem to be required. But they are
necessarily rather rough and ready, and, within limits, other
schemes of division are possible. Our labels are convenient
devices, not revelations from heaven, but it by no means follows
that good reasons cannot be cited for using labels. Nor does it
follow that better reasons may not be found for using one
scheme of division rather than another. As far as the historian
of philosophy is concerned, a good deal depends on his purpose
or aim in writing. But even if the nature of his work leads him
to overstep the limits between traditional periods, he is still
likely to find it necessary to refer to periods.

Reference has been made above simply to traditional divisions between historical periods in the West. But analogous
divisions are made elsewhere. For example, historians refer to
the Middle Ages in Japan; and they are accustomed to make a

division between thought prior and subsequent to the Meiji restoration of 1868. Here again we might make similar remarks to those made above. On the one hand, it would obviously be absurd to imagine that a radical and universal change of thought took place in 1868. On the other hand, the opening of Japan to the West was indubitably an event of great historical importance, and the process of the introduction and growth of influence of western thought, including philosophy, was a real phenomenon.

In connection with the question of division into periods there arises the question of the criteria for distinguishing cultural units. This particular question however becomes acute when we turn our attention to a comparative survey of the philosophies of different cultures, with a view, for example, to ascertaining whether there is any good ground for maintaining that in the philosophical thought of distinct cultures there is a recognizable recurrent pattern. For this sort of enterprise presupposes our ability to identify cultural units. This question however can be left aside here.

6. In his *Autobiography*[37] and later in his *Essay on Metaphysics*[38] R.G. Collingwood maintained that every society has absolute presuppositions of which most people are unconscious, and that it is the task of metaphysics to lay bare and exhibit these absolute presuppositions.[39] In Collingwood's view such presuppositions are neither true nor false. Hence the metaphysician is not called upon to criticize them. His task is simply to discover them. The answers to questions in the theoretical and practical science of any society are propositions of which truth or falsity can be predicated. But this is not the case with the absolute presuppositions lying behind the questions and answers of the sciences, and, indeed, behind the thought and activity of individuals.

Collingwood's contention that the alleged absolute presuppositions are neither true nor false seems to me rather odd. If any of them are formulable as propositions expressing beliefs about reality, it seems to me that they must be qualifiable as true or false. To be sure, if they lie behind all scientific inquiry, we cannot prove that they are true or false. For any proof would presuppose them. And criticism by metaphysicians of the absolute presuppositions of a previous society would presumably be valid only in terms of the absolute presuppositions of their own society. But even if we could not prove the truth or falsity of *p*, it seems to me that *p*, if it expressed a belief about reality, would be either true or false. When Hume maintained that there were 'natural beliefs', the truth of which could not be proved, he did not claim that the beliefs were neither true nor false. He was referring to the limitations of our knowledge. In his view, there might be relatively permanent physical objects, existing independently of impressions; but we could neither prove nor disprove their existence.

However this may be, it is certainly arguable that societies and individuals have their presuppositions. And such presuppositions or assumptions doubtless find expression in philosophies and in philosophical movements. In this case the historian of philosophy is entitled to attempt to exhibit them. In some cases this may be a relatively easy task. For example, there is no great difficulty in mentioning some common presuppositions of medieval society, which influenced medieval philosophy but which could hardly be described as absolute presuppositions in present-day society. In other cases, the task may not be at all so easy to fulfil. When philosophers have tried, for instance, to ascertain and formulate the presuppositions of so-called 'linguistic analysis', they have at once been challenged. It is obviously easier to deal with past societies and philosophies, representatives of which are not to hand to disclaim the presuppositions attributed to them.

Delving into presuppositions is perhaps an enterprise best suited to authors of monographs on particular philosophers or on particular philosophical movements. In a more general history of philosophy serious and prolonged discussion of presuppositions might obscure the story, so to speak. But this is a question of practical considerations. In principle inquiry into presuppositions can hardly be described as irrelevant to an understanding of the historical development of philosophical thought. And the extent, if any, to which the historian introduces this topic must be left, in the first instance, to his judgment. A history which laid emphasis on this line of thought might indeed be enlightening.

7. It seems true to say that in a certain sense philosophy and its history are one and the same thing. For if we understand by philosophy man's activity of philosophizing and if we understand

by history of philosophy the actual development of philosophical thought through the centuries, the two obviously coincide. To say this does not necessarily commit us to a view of the historical development of philosophical thought as a continuous dialectical advance. For nothing is said about advance or progress. It is simply a question of recognizing that the terms 'philosophy' and 'history of philosophy' can be understood in a way which makes them synonymous.

If however we understand by history of philosophy written accounts or reconstructions of the historical development of philosophical thought, and if we prescind from the problem of objectivity, which is still to be considered, we must distinguish between historical accounts of philosophical thought and the actual process of philosophizing. To give an exposition of the critical philosophy of Kant, of his problems, his answers and the process of thought by which he arrived at these answers or solutions is not the same thing as to develop one's own personal treatment of the questions at issue. For one's own view might obviously differ from that of Kant.

The question can therefore be raised, to what extent, if any, is it appropriate for the historian of philosophy to give expression to his own philosophical position? In abstract theory it is possible, I suppose, for someone to write a history of, say, Greek philosophy, using purely conventional criteria of what to include and what to omit, without having any philosophical convictions of his own. But in practice this is an unlikely situation. It is improbable that anyone would undertake the task, unless he had some real interest in philosophy; and he could hardly treat of conflicting theories without having some personal attitude towards the questions at issue. In any case we can ask whether the historian should aim at complete objectivity, in the sense that he should try to give an as objective account as possible of the development of philosophical thought, without letting his own views obtrude themselves at any point, or whether it is appropriate for him to pursue critical discussion of substantive philosophical issues.

It might be argued that the question hardly arises, inasmuch as complete objectivity is an unattainable goal. For one thing, unless the historian slavishly follows some precedent or precedents in regard to what he should include and what he should omit, he exercises personal judgment in selection and emphasis;

and his judgment will inevitably express, even if only implicitly, his own philosophical position. For another thing the historian lives and writes in a certain historical situation and is bound to have a certain perspective, of which of course he may not be aware. Everyone has, and must have, a certain perspective. Hence complete objectivity is not attainable even in principle.

The contention that objectivity is unattainable will be considered in the next chapter. For the moment it is sufficient to remark that in the present context we are not concerned with an objectivity which is alleged to be unattainable in principle. We are concerned with a fairly straightforward common-sense distinction. In some histories of philosophy the writers simply try to explain, for example, what Hume's problems were, how they arose, and how he dealt with them, without either pursuing critical discussion of Hume's philosophy or expressing their own views about the questions at issue. In other histories writers may pursue critical discussion of the philosophical positions of which they give accounts. They may also express their own personal views in regard to the relevant substantive philosophical issues. Whatever we may think about the attainability of an ideal complete objectivity, it is simply an empirical fact that histories of philosophy differ somewhat in the sort of ways just mentioned. And we can quite well ask which course is preferable without involving answers for the moment to the question whether there is a sense in which all historiography inevitably and necessarily is non-objective.

It seems to me that no universally applicable answer to this question can be given. If an historian judges that there is no space available for serious critical discussion, and that it is preferable to omit it altogether rather than to make some comments which he cannot properly develop, how can we legitimately assert that his decision is unjustifiable? If however an historian is convinced that critical discussion would greatly enhance the value of his work as a philosophically educative instrument, he has every right to follow his own judgment. Needless to say, it would be undesirable to write in such a way that the reader was left in serious doubt whether he was reading an exposition of, say, Kant's thought or the historian's reactions to Kant's ideas. Again, we can reasonably demand respect for the distinction between internal and external criticism. It is one thing, for example, to argue, on logical grounds, that a metaphysician's argument is invalid, and it is another thing to criticize metaphysics from the point of view of a logical positivist. Though however we can make a distinction between internal criticism (arguing, for instance, that a certain philosophy contains inconsistencies or even contradictions) and external criticism (such as evaluating a given philosophy from the point of view of a positivist, Marxist, Thomist or what not), and though the former is more appropriate to a history of philosophy, I do not see how we can forbid the latter, namely external criticism, provided that the writer does not try to conceal what he is doing, and provided that the criticism, even if representing a certain philosophical position, takes the form of serious philosophical discussion, and that it is not simply assumed that a given philosopher's view must be wrong if it is incompatible with that of the historian. It is doubtless possible to press the personal element too far. Thus it is arguable that Bertrand Russell's work *A History of Western Philosophy*[40] should have been given some such title as 'My Reactions to a Number of Philosophers'. But even if this work, at any rate in some areas, is remarkably deficient in objectivity, it is certainly entertaining, and it can have a stimulative value.

It is obviously arguable, to perpetrate a tautology, that history is history, and that what is described as a history of philosophy should be just that and nothing more. It should certainly not be a work of propaganda on behalf of Marxism, Thomism, positivism, existentialism, or what not. But is it really necessary that a history of philosophy should be either simply expository and exegetical or a work of propaganda in a pejorative sense? If, for example, a neo-Wittgensteinian wrote a history of modern western philosophy and criticized the logical-positivist criterion of meaning from the point of view of someone who accepted Wittgenstein's attitude as expressed in *Philosophical Investigations*, he could in some sense be said to be conducting propaganda for a certain position. But provided that he gave a fair and objective account of the logical-positivist thesis and of the reasons why it was proposed, and provided that his critical discussion was properly philosophical, it would hardly be a case of propaganda in a sense in which propaganda is something to be avoided.[41] For my own part, I am inclined to think that critical discussion in a work which is explicitly a history of philosophy is best confined to internal criticism. But I am not prepared to assert that an historian should never show his hand, so to speak. I would only remark that if he does this, he should do it, show his hand that is to say, and not at the same time lay claim to an absolute neutrality.

The word 'criticism' ordinarily suggests the idea of adverse criticism. But this is not necessarily the case. A literary critic might give a favourable evaluation of a work. And critical discussion of successive philosophies might be directed to finding the truth in each. This procedure might involve the assumption that each philosophy *must* embody a truth which is a phase in the development of philosophy itself, the one perennial philosophy which develops in and through the succession of movements and systems. We would then have the sort of approach represented by Hegel. Hegel's approach to the history of philosophy however rests on certain metaphysical premises. And though he is free to assume these premises, they are open to question. Besides, Hegel's lectures on the history of philosophy are clearly an integral part of a philosophical system, namely absolute idealism. It is not simply a case of an historian judging the arguments and conclusions of philosophers in the light of his own philosophical convictions. The metaphysical premises seem to influence the actual historical account. For it is assumed that man's philosophizing is the process by which the Absolute or Reality or the Universe considered as the One realizes self-consciousness. And a belief of this kind can hardly help affecting selection and emphasis. In order however to pursue the policy of looking for the truth in every philosophy it is not necessary to assume, for metaphysical reasons, that successive philosophies *must* embody successive phases of developing truth. It is sufficient to assume that it is more probable than not that an original philosopher sees some facet of truth, even if he then exaggerates its significance or shows himself to be myopic in regard to other aspects of truth. This seems to be a quite reasonable assumption or working hypothesis.

While however the historian is free to approach his subject in this way, it can be objected that what the historian takes to be the truth is what seems to him to be the truth, that what seems to him to be truth is determined by his perspective, and that it is idle for him to try to pass himself off as an impartial spectator and judge. This line of thought brings us back to an aspect of the problem of objectivity, to which we can now turn, though it may well be preferable to speak of problems of objectivity rather than of *the* problem of objectivity, as though there were only one.

Notes

[1] *Summa Theologiae,1a*, cf. q.1, a.1, reply to obj. 2.

[2] We can say that, for Aquinas, the existence of God was a premise in Christian theology and a conclusion in metaphysics. In his view philosophy culminated in the limited knowledge of God attainable by the human mind by inference from premises, the truth of which was known by the natural light of reason.

[3] It is possible to object to Aquinas's account of 'sacred doctrine' on the ground that it implies a propositional theory of revelation, and that this theory is open to criticism. But this is not the point at issue. The point is that Aquinas provides a way of distinguishing between Christian theology and philosophy, which would not confine all talk about God to the former.

[4] In, for example, his work *A Short History of Chinese Philosophy*, edited by Derk Bodde (New York, 1960).

[5] It is not my intention to suggest that Yu-Lan intended his distinction to be understood in such a way as to have this implication.

[6] I refer to Artistotle's conception of numbers and so on as belonging to the sphere of 'the unmoved' (in the sense that the mathematician, unlike the physicist, is not treating of changing or moving bodies) and the non-separate (in the sense that though numbers, triangles and so on are conceived in abstraction from matter, they do not exist separately, in the way in which Aristotle believed that the intelligences of the spheres existed).

[7] Needless to say, an historian is entitled, if he wishes, to select a limited field, say the development of empiricism or the rise of positivism. This procedure would be quite different from writing what purported to be a general history of philosophy in a certain period and then omitting prominent features of the philosophy in question.

[8] Both Śamkhara and Spinoza had in mind explicit recognition of an already existing relation between the human soul and the Absolute. They were not thinking of an ontological relationship which did not yet exist and had to be brought into being for the first time, so to speak.

[9] In the *Tractatus Theologico-Politicus* Spinoza makes it clear that in his view the Bible is concerned not with truth but with piety and obedience, and that truth is the aim of philosophy.

[10] Some work has been done in this field. See, for example, *Ways of Thinking of Eastern Peoples* by Hajime Nakamura (East-West Center Press, Honolulu, 1964). But we are really only at the beginning of specialized studies.

[11] It is possible of course for an historian of philosophy to go simply by what is required for practical purposes: e.g., to provide students with the material required to pass fairly undemanding examinations. But I am talking about an historian who is genuinely concerned with the historical development of philosophical thinking. He must obviously have an idea of what is to count as philosophical thinking, an idea which he could, if asked, support with reasons other than those of pure expediency.

[12] Of this work we possess only part of the treatise 'On Sensation', published as *'De sensu'* by Hermann Diels in *Doxographi Graeci* (Berlin, 1879).

[13] This work, together with an English translation, is included, in two volumes, in the Loeb Classical Library (London & New York, 1925). There is a critical edition in two volumes by H.S. Long, *Diogenis Laërtii Vitae Philosophorum* (Oxford, 1964). As Diogenes Laërtius omits any treatment of Neoplatonism, it is assumed that he wrote early in the third century AD.

[14] The 1886 Tübingen edition was reprinted in 1964 (Frankfurt am M. & New York).

[15] A Latin translation appeared at Amsterdam in 1690, and there were subsequent editions at Leipzig and Venice.

[16] The first edition (Leipzig, 1742-44) comprised five volumes. The second edition (1766-67) was in six volumes.

[17] These remarks about Scholastic textbooks may perhaps be considered unfair. For the authors were concerned with the elements of Scholastic philosophy rather than with the history of philosophy. It is undeniable however that philosophers of whose views the authors disapproved were often caricatured, inasmuch as the opinions or conclusions, considered without reference to context, actual problematics and the relevant lines of thought, often seemed bizarre or absurd. Happily, this way of treating eminent thinkers has disappeared from Thomist writing.

[18] Wilhelm Windelband's *Lehrbuch der Geschichte der Philosophie* (1892) was translated into English as *History of Philosophy* by J.N. Tufts (New York, 1893; second edition, 1901). A revised edition by H. Heimsoeth appeared at Tübingen in 1948.

[19] There have indeed been some long-lived schools in the West, or at any rate schools which have had a new lease of life. Thomism is an example. This has been due very largely to the association of a school with an extra-philosophical factor. One might perhaps find an analogy in the persistence of the traditions of, say, Buddhist sects.

[20] A group of Indian philosophers, who were envisaging a new history of Indian philosophy, once spoke to me in conversation about the relative lack of knowledge about chronological sequences in early Indian thought. The implication was that they would like, if possible, to give greater prominence to individuals and the relations between them.

[21] *The Tragic Sense of Life in Men and Nations*, section 1. In the translation by J.E. Crawford Flitch (London, 1921) the passage occurs on p. 2, while in the translation by A. Kenigan (Princeton University Press & London, 1972) it occurs on p. 4.

[22] *Wittgenstein*, by W.W. Bartley (Philadelphia & New York, 1973).

[23] See, for example, *The Life of Bertrand Russell*, by Ronald W. Clark (London, 1975), p. 172.

[24] As I have indicated, I do not know whether this was the case or not. I simply make an assumption to illustrate a point. In any case to be subject to homosexual inclinations is no crime.

[25] It is true that Nietzsche looked for empirical confirmation of the theory in question, which implies that he regarded it as an empirical hypothesis. But if we consider the way in which the idea first came to him and his comments on the experience, it is pretty clear that the theory was basically intended as a test of strength and was judged from an evaluative point of view. Again, the theory of *Übermensch* (Superman or, as Americans are inclined to translate, Overman) is not, in my opinion, an addition, so to speak, to Darwinism, but rather a myth, a spur to the will. In this case it is otiose to ask whether it is true or false, or whether there is sufficient evidence to support the hypothesis.

[26] At this point I am simply assuming that there are 'recurrent tendencies', without further discussion.

[27] I say 'in theory at least' inasmuch as I have encountered this idea or suggestion in monographs on individual thinkers rather than in general histories of philosophy. See, for example, R. Wollheim's book on F.H. Bradley (*F.H. Bradley*, Harmondsworth, 1959).

[28] It does not follow that there was no genuine philosophical thought in the medieval period, but only theology. If X influences Y, it does not follow that Y is X.

[29] I am thinking, for example, of what is sometimes called inductive metaphysics, a concept of metaphysics which represents metaphysical theories as hypo-

theses and thus has to find something analogous to empirical testing.

[30] I am not suggesting that there is any necessary clash, or even tension, between science and religion. But there can certainly be a tension between a scientific outlook or mentality (if preferred, a 'scientistic' mentality) and a religious vision of the universe. This tension can exist in the form of a tension or clash between the outlooks of different persons. But it can also exist within one and the same person.

[31] The thought of John Locke exercised an influence, directly or indirectly, on the minds of some of those responsible for the American Declaration of Independence. But it would be an obvious exaggeration to ascribe the American Revolution to the political thought of Locke. His thought was simply a contributing factor, though a real one.

[32] There are some remarks on this subject in my *History of Philosophy*, Vol. 7, pp. 13-21. I do not wish to repeat them here.

[33] For one thing, a certain measure of perspectivism on the part of the author seems to be inevitable.

[34] It is obviously open to critics to challenge the historian's judgment.

[35] A book was once published in which Berkeley's philosophical ideas were related, in an ingenious manner, to his chronic constipation. But I know of no firm evidence that the good bishop suffered from chronic constipation in the first place. How far this theory was intended seriously, I do not know.

[36] This phrase is open to serious objections. For all thought is thought by persons. But the term can none the less be given meaning. For example, we can distinguish between a thinker whose philosophy cannot be properly understood without reference to the man and his life and a thinker whose philosophy can more easily be considered apart from any reference to 'inner biography'.

[37] London, 1939.

[38] Oxford, 1940.

[39] Collingwood claimed to have already set out this sort of theory in the manuscript of *Truth and Reconstruction*. But this manuscript was rejected by a publisher in 1917, and Collingwood destroyed it when he had written his *Autobiography*.

[40] *A History of Western Philosophy: its Connection with Political and Social Circumstances from the Earliest Times to the Present Day* (London & New York, 1945). It is only in some particular cases that Russell makes any serious attempt to exhibit the connection between philosophy and its political and social milieu.

[41] The word 'propaganda' is generally used in a pejorative sense, it is true. But it could be used to refer to promotion of a certain view, when the promotion was carried on by honest and serious discussion. In a religious context, 'propagation of the faith' need not involve playing on the ambiguity of terms, using sophistical arguments, caricaturing the beliefs of others, and so on.

CHAPTER II

PROBLEMS OF OBJECTIVITY

The past as non-existent — datum and interpretation — selection and emphasis — the historian and the perspective of his time.

1. The historian, it may be said, is concerned with what does not exist. For his subject-matter is the past; and, by definition, the past is not the present, and so no longer exists. To be sure, the historian tries to reconstruct the past; and his reconstruction exists in the present. But we are not in a position to compare the reconstruction with a non-existent original. Even if therefore the reconstruction happens to be an objective representation of the past, we cannot know that it is. And what holds good for historiography in general also holds good for the history of philosophy in particular. David Hume lived and thought and wrote in the eighteenth century. He is long since dead. The historian of British philosophy tries to interpret his mind, to reconstruct his thought; but we have no access to Hume's mind. We cannot check the accuracy of the historian's reconstruction. It may conceivably be a faithful or objective reconstruction; but, even if it is, we cannot know that this is the case.

Obviously, this line of thought implies that we are really unable to distinguish between history and fiction. It is equally obvious that this is not a conclusion which most of us are prepared to accept. That is to say, we spontaneously feel that there must be something wrong with any argument which implies the conclusion in question. We are convinced, for example, that it is possible to distinguish between an historical account of the life and death of King Charles I and an entertaining piece of fiction in which the author recounts how some devoted subject took the monarch's place on the scaffold and how Charles started a new life abroad.

It is doubtless true that if we were challenged, many of us would be unable to produce further evidence to support our belief that Charles I was beheaded than the testimony of historians. And it might be claimed that to appeal to such testimony is naive. For if the objectivity of historiography, or, more precisely, an ability to establish its objectivity, has been called in question, it is no good trying to show that we can indeed make historical statements which we know to be objectively true by appealing to the fact that all the relevant historians make a certain assertion. If somebody called in question the general belief that there are relatively permanent physical objects or things, existing independently of our impressions, sense-data or what not, it would hardly be an adequate reply if we were to retort that there is a general belief in the existence of physical objects. For it would be precisely the validity of this belief which had been questioned. Similarly, what the historians may say is no guarantee of an ability to distinguish between objective history and fiction. For it is precisely what they think and say which has been challenged.

An obvious retort to this line of thought is that though the past, by definition, does not exist, it none the less did exist, also by definition. And there can perfectly well be evidence of what existed but no longer exists. Conan Doyle wrote a well-known novel about the discovery of living dinosaurs, pterodactyls and so on in an hitherto unexplored part of South America. We all recognize this as a work of fiction, and we would not ask for evidence that Professor Challenger actually made the discoveries in question. In the case however of what purports to be an historical account of past events one can sensibly ask for evidence. In practice we obviously tend to accept the word of historians, at any rate when they agree, as we assume that they know the facts and that they are not lying or attempting to deceive us. But this does not alter the fact that in the case of what are claimed to be true historical statements it is appropriate in principle to ask for the evidence, whereas it would be inappropriate to ask for evidence that Sherlock Holmes smoked a pipe. The only 'evidence' required is Conan Doyle's description. In the case however of the statement that King Charles I was beheaded it is not simply a matter of all the historians saying that he was beheaded. Ultimately the assertion rests on evidence, even if in practice some historians may accept the statement on the word of other historians, as they know of no good reason to doubt its veracity. If necessary, the evidence can be produced.

To turn to history of philosophy. It is obviously true that David Hume is long since dead. But his writings exist in the present, and it is with these that the historian of British philosophy is chiefly concerned. If Hume's writings had entirely perished, and if there were no other reliable testimony to his thought, it is clear that a reconstruction of his thought would be indistinguishable from fiction. For we cannot interrogate or listen to a man who died in 1776. In this sense we have no access to his mind. But in another sense we have such access, for his mind is expressed in his writings, and these exist in the present. There is of course the bare logical possibility that Hume was pulling a fast one on his readers, and that he did not really mean what he said. But the burden of proof lies on the shoulders of anyone who proposes such a hypothesis. For the available evidence supports the view that Hume was concerned with expressing his real mind, except for those writings or passages in which he was clearly observing a measure of prudent discretion and left his own attitude somewhat obscure. In point of fact the situation is not substantially different from what it would be, if Hume had been alive today. It is logically possible that a living or contemporary philosopher is lying or that he is concealing rather than expressing his personal convictions. But the burden of proof lies on the shoulders of the person who suggests that in his published works a philosopher intends to deceive his reading public and that he really holds convictions opposed to those which he presents as his own in his writings.

The resolute sceptic will not indeed allow himself to be persuaded by such considerations. He may say, for example, that talk about evidence is all very well, but that evidence is what we decide to treat as evidence. Again, what we call evidence is often ambiguous and can be used to support different conclusions. One person decides to treat the evidence as pointing to conclusion *a*, while someone else decides to treat it as pointing to conclusion *b*. Further, if evidence is supposed to have a relation to the past, does not this mean that it has a relation to the non-existent?

It is clear, I think, that before something can be cited as evidence it has to be recognized as evidence. Its evidential value, or its possible evidential value, has to be seen or appreciated. And I suppose that it might be said that we 'decide' to treat something as evidence, in the sense that we make up our minds that it is evidence, or to recognize it as such. But it by no means follows that one's decision to treat something as evidence is a purely arbitrary decision. For example, it is not simply a matter of arbitrary choice if we treat Aristotle's remarks about early Greek philosophers as evidence of their views and theories. To be sure, Aristotle, like other people, could make mistakes or misinterpret people's statements. And we have to allow for a tendency to interpret the ideas of predecessors in terms of a process of preparation for Aristotle's own philosophy. The fact remains however that in some cases Aristotle was in a much better position than we are to know what was held by his predecessors. When possible, we obviously have to evaluate Aristotle's account in the light of fragments and of other accounts. And there may still remain a good deal of obscurity and uncertainty. But this does not alter the fact that Aristotle had access to a good deal of literature which is no longer extant. To use his statements as contributory evidence about earlier Greek philosophy is not the result of an arbitrary decision. The decision is a reasoned one, or at any rate one that can be supported by reasons.

As for the objection that what is called evidence can be ambiguous, this is doubtless true. That is to say, it sometimes happens that the evidential significance of x can be interpreted in more than one way. But this does not affect the fact that in some other cases it can be reasonably interpreted only as supporting a certain definite belief or statement. There is, for example, evidence that on a certain date British rule in India ceased. And the relevant documents and records cannot reasonably be interpreted as supporting a different belief or conclusion.

What about the questions whether evidence is supposed to have a relation to the past, and, if so, whether this does not mean that it has a relation to the non-existent? It can be pointed out in the first place that to recognize something as evidence, a document, say, or an archaeological find, is to relate it to the past, in the sense that it is recognized as a ground for making a certain statement about the past. In the second place, when we make a positive statement about the past, it is misleading to say simply that we are making a statement about the non-existent. We are asserting that something did exist or that

something did occur. Suppose that we make an historical statement about the Roman empire. The Roman empire does not
exist now. But we are saying something about it as existing in
the past or about it as it was when it existed. The evidence for
our statement is related to the Roman empire as existing, in the
sense that it is or is deemed to be sufficient ground for making a
statement in the present about the empire as existing in the
past. There is no need at all to think of there being a relation, as
a real entity, one term of which is what we describe as evidence,
while the other term is the non-existent, in the sense of not-
being or nothingness.

Perhaps what the sceptic is looking for or demanding is a logical demonstration that we can have objective historical knowledge, at any rate by proving, beyond the logical possibility of
error, that one or more historical statements are objectively
true. If so, he seems to be demanding what cannot be given.
One might just as well refuse to accept any scientific hypothesis, unless its truth could be proved in such a way as to exclude
the logical possibility of any alternative hypothesis being true.
The attitudes seem to be analogous at any rate if both scientific
hypotheses and historical statements are revisable in principle.
But it no more follows that all historical statements are equally
uncertain than it follows that all scientific hypotheses are
equally open to doubt. Historians have stronger evidence for
some of their statements than they have for others. Sometimes
they may fill in gaps between events, the occurrence of which is
well supported by evidence, by saying what, in their opinion,
most probably happened. And if an historian chooses to refer to
people's motives and intentions, even when the agent has not
stated them, there is obviously bound to be an element of conjecture. But this does not alter the fact that for some historical
statements we have evidence which would be rejected only by
someone who was looking for what, by the nature of the subject-matter, cannot be provided. If I am asked to prove that
there is a piece of paper here, I may be able to make explicit
some at least of the reasons which I have for believing that there
is a piece of paper here. But if all such reasons are rejected and I
am asked to give a quasi-mathematical demonstration of the
existence of the paper, I can only reply that it is not a question
of mathematics and that the demand should not be made. Analogously, evidence can be mentioned to support the statement

that the last Russian Tsar and Tsarina were murdered on a certain date and at a certain place. If one cannot demonstrate this historical fact in such a way as to exclude the logical possibility of the imperial couple having survived and having continued their lives in absolute secrecy, this does not alter the fact that there is sound evidence of the assassination. It is logically possible, I suppose, that Queen Victoria is still alive and is working somewhere as an extremely elderly barmaid; but nobody in his senses refuses to accept the evidence of her death.

To apply these remarks to the history of philosophy. The fact that there is always a logical possibility of error in the historian's interpretation of a past philosopher's mind seems to be irrelevant. As has been already remarked, historians are not infallible. But there are none the less checks on what they say. The strength of the checks differs in different cases. We cannot be as confident of an insight into the mind of Thales as we may be of an insight into the mind of, say, Berkeley or J.S. Mill. And even in this case our confidence may sometimes be unwarranted. But even if historians differ somewhat in their interpretations, there is at any rate evidence to appeal to. And it seems absurd to suggest that a serious account of the thought of Berkeley or of Mill or of Bertrand Russell is indistinguishable from a purely fictional representation of an imagined philosopher and his imagined theories. The fallibility of historians, including historians of philosophy, no more makes them indistinguishable from writers of historical fiction than the fallibility of scientists warrants the conclusion that they are indistinguishable from writers of science fiction.

It is hardly necessary to say that in practice even the sceptic assumes that we can know some historical facts. He does not proceed on the assumption that the first world war is a fiction invented by self-styled historians or that, if it really occurred, we cannot know that it occurred. It is no longer occurring; and in this sense it does not exist. Apart however from the raising of theoretical puzzles, the sceptic makes the same sort of assumptions that other people make. The problem, as I have depicted it in this section, is therefore likely to seem to most readers unrealistic or sophistical. And I have argued that it does in fact leave out or pass over in silence aspects of the situation which should be borne in mind. As far as the history of philosophy is concerned, it is very misleading to suggest that historians are concerned with what does not exist. For they are primarily concerned with what certainly does exist, namely, the writings of philosophers, in some cases fragments of these writings, and with extant records or reports of their thought. To be sure, the historian tries to elucidate not simply what the writings, taken purely by themselves, might conceivably mean but what was meant by their authors. And, unless the historian includes living people, the authors are dead and cannot be asked for elucidation. Hence there is room, within limits, for different lines of interpretation. But this does not alter the fact that there can be varying degrees of evidence, providing stronger or weaker grounds as the case may be, for the statements made by historians. There can be no reasonable doubt, for example, that Kant moved from a pre-critical to a critical stage in his thought, though, within limits, there can be reasonable doubt about the correct interpretation of some of his theories. The limits are set by the writings themselves and by what we may know from other sources about Kant's mind. The writings exist, and they give us access, even if not complete access, to Kant's mind, despite the fact that he is no longer about.

As the line of sceptical objection, as stated and considered in this section, tends to seem contrived and, to many people, unrealistic and sophistical, I now wish to turn to a less contrived manner of raising the problem of historical objectivity. I refer to the question of distinguishing between data and interpretation.

2. If someone sets out to write a biography of a well-known historical figure, a politician for example, he has to assemble his material, such as facts relating to his subject's upbringing and education, his introduction to political life, his speeches, letters written by and to him, records of friendships, quarrels and enmities, the measures which he advocated, what he actually achieved in this or that ministerial post, and so on. Though however the biographer requires and utilizes such material, his task is obviously something more than publishing a collection of facts, reports, correspondence, speeches, and so forth. He has to tell a connected story which expresses his evaluation of the significance of the data. And in doing so he is bound to interpret. To be sure, he may abstain from making judgments about, say, the politician's 'real' motives and goals, as distinct from his pro-

fessed ideals. None the less the material is likely to be presented in such a way that the attentive reader will draw or at least consider certain conclusions. In any case the biographer will depict the man and his life in the way which he thinks most in accordance with the data and factual evidence. In fine, it is natural to make a distinction between data or facts and their interpretation. After all, different biographers may give rather different interpretations of the life of a certain individual, even if one biographer does not know more facts than the other and does not deny that what the other admits as facts really are facts.

The biographer bears some resemblance to the portrait painter who is not content simply to photograph but who interprets what he sees. We naturally think of the sitter as being the same for all observers. But different portrait painters can convey different impressions of the same sitter. The sitter, we might say, is the datum; but the interpretations of the datum may differ.

In the field of history of philosophy too it is natural to make a distinction between material or data on the one hand and evaluation and interpretation of the data on the other, and to think that while the former are, so to speak, neutral and the same for all, the latter may differ somewhat. For example, even if two historians are in agreement not only about which of the dialogues traditionally attributed to Plato are authentic but also about the chronological order in which the dialogues were composed, their presentations of Plato's thought may differ considerably. Again, agreement that Locke, Berkeley and Hume wrote certain works does not necessarily mean that presentations of the development of classical British empiricism will be precisely similar. Nor does agreement about the written material or data provided by the Young Hegelians entail agreement about the most significant and important aspects of the movement of thought in question. If one interprets the Young Hegelians in terms of the relation between them and Marx, one's picture of the movement is likely to be rather different from what it would be if one paid little attention to Marx's reactions and concentrated instead on what Feuerbach, for instance, considered important. In other words, the same data can be looked at from different perspectives; and interpretations of the data will differ accordingly.

If this distinction is pressed, it seems to imply that the historian of philosophy is concerned with the interpretation of bare facts, of data, that is to say, which are themselves free of interpretation. But, it can be asked, is this implication acceptable? It may seem reasonable to claim that Kant's *Critique of the Pure Reason* constitutes a datum for the historian, in the sense that it is part of the material which he regards as given, about which he reflects, and which he includes in his account of the development of philosophical thought. Though however this claim is valid up to a point, inasmuch as Kant's first *Critique* is for the historian something given and not something which he creates or composes, what precisely constitutes the datum for reflection? It is surely not the first *Critique* considered simply as a physical object. For the historian could not reflect on the work, relate it to Kant's other writings, exhibit the problems which it attempts to answer, try to elucidate its obscurities, assess its influence and so on, unless he had performed an activity of reading which itself involves interpretation. We might perhaps speak of the work, considered as a physical object, as a potential datum. But it becomes the actual datum on which the historian reflects only through its being seen as a philosophical work and being subjected to interpretation.

In the present context this line of thought is envisaged as a ground for casting doubt on the objectivity of the history of philosophy. It could obviously be extended to apply to all historiography. The contention is that the historian has no bare facts or uninterpreted data to work on. In this case the picture which he paints is his construction, and it cannot be checked by referring to neutral or uninterpreted data, if there are no such data. It can indeed be criticized; but then it is criticized in the light of someone else's perspective, of another interpretation. Historians are human beings; and as far as human beings are concerned, there is no absolute perspective. For the data to which the historian appeals are themselves interpretations and fall under a certain perspective. There are no data which are uncoloured, as it were, by any perspective.

If this argument is pressed, it appears to follow that, as Nietzsche maintained, there are only perspectives. That is to say, we cannot indicate what they are perspectives of. We cannot say what an historian's interpretation is an interpretation of, if there are no uninterpreted data, no neutral or bare facts to which we can appeal. If therefore historian *A* criticizes an interpretation given by historian *B*, he does so in terms of his own, *A*'s, interpretation. And if the claim that historiography can be objective involves belief in the possibility of attaining an absolute and non-perspectival vision, the claim is bogus.

The thesis that there are no facts but only interpretations is likely to seem to most people to be contrary to common sense. For must not an interpretation be an interpretation of something? Let us suppose, for example, that Tom gave Jack a violent push in the presence of a number of witnesses. Does not common sense suggest that this is a basic fact which must be distinguished from the various possible ways of interpreting it? Did Tom slip on something and push Jack without really intending to? Or was Tom trying to push Jack out of the way of an oncoming car? Or (a possible interpretation in some places) did Tom catch sight of a man with a gun which he was just about to fire and give Jack a violent push to get him out of the probable line of fire? Again, physical scientists can be said to interpret the world. But can we seriously suppose that their interpretations are not interpretations of anything, and that science is knowledge of a fictional world?

Though however it certainly seems to be in accordance with common sense to say that it is a fact that Tom gave Jack a violent push or shove, a fact of which there might be different possible interpretations, is not the factual statement itself an interpretation of the phenomena? The witnesses describe what they saw; and to describe is to interpret. Again, while it is natural to think of scientists as interpreting the world, is not the concept of 'the world' itself an interpretation?

What are we to say about all this? It seems to the present writer that each side has a valid point to make, and that one should attempt to combine these points. Let us start with the common-sense attitude.

The distinction between data and interpretation certainly seems to be justified, if it is understood in a relative sense. For example, we can reasonably claim that in comparison with more or less probable assessments of Stalin's motives in liquidating Bukharin in 1938 it is a firm historical fact that Stalin was responsible for Bukharin's trial and execution. To say this does not mean that the logical possibility of error is excluded. It means that for certain statements, such as 'Bukharin was executed in 1938', the evidence is such that, in the absence of any fresh evidence to the contrary, no sensible person would reject it. In assessing Stalin's motives however there is room for conjecture: there can be rather different interpretations which are comparable with the available evidence. For practical purposes therefore we can take Bukharin's execution and Stalin's responsibility for it as data for interpretation. An analogous case would be the situation in a criminal law court, when the members of the jury are expected to take as data for reflection facts which have been established in such a way that they are questioned neither by the prosecution nor by the defence.

Consider one or two examples from the history of philosophy. If historians A, B and C are all agreed that certain dialogues attributed to Plato are authentic, the statement that he regarded the soul as having three parts can be taken by them as a datum. But it by no means follows that their interpretations of this statement are precisely the same. Again, unless we are prepared to question the authenticity of the writings attributed to Berkeley, it is plain as a pikestaff that he asserted that sensible things are ideas. This assertion can thus be regarded as a datum. But how precisely the assertion should be understood is, within limits, a matter for discussion; and there can be somewhat different interpretations.

The common-sense point of view is therefore justified up to a point. That is to say, we can make a pragmatically useful distinction between data and interpretations, and we can explain our need for it. If every historian of British empiricism had to do all the spade-work over again and could not take certain things as data or established facts, he would not get very far. It does not necessarily follow however that the distinction between historical data and interpretations is absolute. For example, in relation to somewhat different interpretations of Berkeley's philosophy we can take it as a given fact that he asserted that sensible things are ideas. But this fact is itself the expression of an interpretation of symbols. To establish the fact we have to read and understand the symbols, to interpret them. Again, though we can indeed take it as fact, as an historical datum, that Stalin was responsible for Bukharin's execution, the statement that he was so responsible is itself the result of interpretation. Further, what would generally be described as an interpretation might be converted into a datum, in the sense indicated. For instance, some historians have defended a theistic interpretation of Hegel's doctrine of the Absolute. Other historians think that this interpretation is untenable. Suppose that we discovered a paper or a letter by Hegel, written in his maturity, in which he gave a clear and unambiguous account of his theory of the Absolute and put it beyond dispute that self-consciousness or self-awareness could not be attributed to the Absolute in itself, independently, that is to say, of the human mind. The theistic interpretation would then be excluded, and we might reasonably take it as an historical fact or datum that Hegel was not a theist. The establishment of this fact would obviously be itself the result of interpretation; but in relation to remaining disputable questions and interpretations it could none the less be treated as a datum. Conversely, what has for long been considered an historical fact can sometimes turn out to be doubtful or even not a fact at all.

The question at issue seems to be this. If the distinction between datum and interpretation is assumed to be relative, with the consequence that there are no hard and fast data, does it follow that historiography is a purely subjective construction, or at any rate that if an historical account happens to be objectively true, we cannot know that it is? This conclusion is obviously not one which we are prepared to accept and act on in practice. For we are convinced that we can distinguish between different historical statements in terms of the quality of the evidence for their truth. For example, the evidence is such that we cannot reasonably doubt that Stalin was responsible for the execution of Bukharin. But, as far as I know, the evidence is not strong enough to warrant a definite assertion that at one period of his life Stalin worked for the Okhrana, the Tsarist secret police. The available evidence might, it appears, be interpreted in somewhat different ways. Again, while the evidence is quite sufficient to warrant the assertion that Plotinus held certain theories, the influence on his mind of Eastern thought is, though possible, a matter for conjecture. Though however we can get along all right in practice (that is, though we can in practice distinguish degrees of evidential support for historical statements), theoretical problems or puzzles can still be raised. Thus it can be asked whether evidence is or is not reducible, in the long run, to hard data or bare facts; and the claim may be made that if it is not so reducible, the evidence itself is infected with subjectivity, and the original problem, instead of being solved, is simply pushed further back. After all, evidence has to be interpreted as evidence. From one point of view an archaeological find, for example, is simply what it is; it says nothing about the past. If we claim that it does, this is because we interpret it as revealing something about the past. And the interpretation is a construction of the human mind, the mind of the interpreter that is to say.

There are various possible ways of dealing with this sort of puzzle or problem. One way is to dismiss it as unrealistic and superfluous. In face of the demand for a theoretical justification of scientific inference from the known to the unknown, some philosophers have maintained that no such justification is needed. The only justification is a pragmatic one. If scientific inference works, if its predictions are verified, no further justification is required. Analogously, it can be maintained that as we can in practice distinguish between evidentially warranted historical statements and statements which express more or less reasonable (or even unreasonable) conjectures, it is a waste of time to worry about theoretical puzzles which really leave historiography precisely where it was before. If this attitude seems too cavalier, it can be added that the sceptic is really demanding what cannot, by the nature of the case, be obtained. What he is really looking for, before he is prepared to admit the existence of historical knowledge, is exclusion of the logical possibility of error. If however all historical statements are in principle revisable, we cannot exclude the logical possibility of error. Nor do we need to do so. It is logically possible that Charles I was not beheaded. For it is logically possible that those who recorded the beheading were lying, or that a substitution was successfully effected. Such logical possibilities however are so improbable that for all practical purposes we can take it as certain that the monarch's head was cut off. To demand more than a very high degree of probability is, in effect, to confuse historiography with a formal science such as mathematics.

To dismiss the puzzle may however seem a case of evading a real problem. And an attempt may be made to show that in the long run historical statements are in fact reducible to immediate data of experience which are not themselves interpretations. Thus we can try to reduce historical statements to sense-data.

There are however familiar objections to this procedure. Consider the statement that William the Conqueror landed in England in 1066. It is true of course that if this event really occurred, then, given certain necessary conditions (such as having reasonable eyesight) those who were present would have seen William landing or, if such a way of speaking is permissible, would have had certain sense-data. But it seems difficult to maintain successfully that a statement about William the Conqueror is reducible or equivalent to a statement or set of statements about the sense-data of other people. Further, how do we know that some people in 1066 had certain sense-data? It may be said that the statement about William is equivalent to hypothetical sense-data rather than to actual ones. But this thesis is somewhat perplexing. Again, though one might be prepared to admit that the hearing of a bang can be considered an immediate datum of experience, provided that one does not assign a cause (such as a tyre bursting, a bomb exploding, or what not), if one reports the experience, one might misdescribe it. If I do not know English well or if I am given to confusing words, I might say 'I heard a bang' when, according to linguistic convention, I ought to have used other terms. In other words, the possibility of error does not seem to be really excluded by interpreting historical statements in terms of sense-data.

Another possible way of coping with the matter is to have recourse to phenomenology and to claim that the demand for bare data of experience is quite unjustified, inasmuch as there is and cannot be any such thing. That is to say, anything which can be described as a datum of experience must be seen *as* something. If I see an object in a wood in the dusk, I may be uncertain whether it is a man or the stump of a tree; but even then I see it *as* something, namely as an object with a certain general appearance, distinct from its environment, an object which may turn out to be a man or a tree stump. Analogously, if a person witnesses an accident in the street, he experiences it *as* an accident in the street. He does not first experience a lot of detached sense-data and then infer the occurrence of an accident. And when we read a dialogue of Plato, we experience it, if we understand it at all, *as* a philosophical work. If therefore we can describe experiencing-*as* as interpretation, it follows that there can be no experience without interpretation. And in this case it is foolish to demand uninterpreted experiential data before we are prepared to admit that historiography is not a purely subjective construction. Knowledge is a relation between subject and object; and there must be contributions, so to speak, from both sides.

It is, I think, true that if by a datum of experience we mean an object of consciousness or awareness, it must be experienced *as* something. This idea might perhaps be said to lie at the basis of Kantian theory. Even if we reject Kant's account of the *a priori* elements in knowledge, it is reasonable to claim that its general implication is that whatever we experience, we experience *as* having some characteristic or characteristics or as being an object of a certain kind.

Mention of Kant can however be misleading. For it may suggest the idea that when we see X as a, the a-ness is a subjective contribution, a veil, so to speak, with which the subject clothes an unknown, and indeed unknowable X. But to claim that to see X is to see it as a or b or c, is not necessarily to imply that X is not a or b or c. Why should it? I am aware of an object lying on my table. I see it as a pencil. It by no means follows that the object is not a pencil. It is reasonable to claim that the people who were present at the beheading of King Charles I saw the course of events as the beheading of the king. It by no means follows that this was a purely subjective interpretation or reading of the events. Two people look at the Greek text of a dialogue of Plato. One of them, knowing no Greek and being entirely ignorant who Plato was, sees the text as a succession of symbols or characters to which he can attach no significance, as a text which he cannot understand. The other man sees it as a philosophical work. It obviously does not follow that the dialogue is not a philosophical work.

Though however the claim that every datum of experience is experienced *as* something does not entail the conclusion that the object is not what it is seen as being, neither does it entail the conclusion that the logical possibility of error can be excluded. It is indeed arguable that I cannot be mistaken about my immediate sense-data. I cannot be mistaken in seeing a white patch as a white patch. But it can also be argued that I may misdescribe the immediate object of awareness. Perhaps I use the word 'white' when, according to linguistic convention, I should use the word 'green'. And this applies to what I say to myself no less than to what I say to others. If however we leave the sense-datum theory out of account, it seems clear that when I see X as a, I may conceivably be mistaken. I see the object on my table as a pencil. And this is what it most probably is. But it is logically possible that a colleague has substituted for my pencil an object which looks at first sight like a pencil but is really not one and is quite incapable of fulfilling the functions of a pencil. It is logically conceivable that the people who believed that they were witnessing the beheading of Charles I were mistaken, and that they were really seeing the beheading of a substitute for the monarch. As for the dialogue of Plato, a distinction may be appropriate. On the assumption that the object really is one of the Platonic dialogues, it may be said to follow by definition that it is a philosophical work. But if the text is simply labelled *Phaedo* or *Theaetetus* and I see it as a philosophical work, I may be mistaken. It might be a comedy of Aristophanes which has been given a misleading label or title.

The fact however that error is possible when I see X as a does not entail the conclusion that the error, if there is one, cannot be cleared up. I see the object on my table as a pencil. I may conceivably be mistaken. But if I pick up the object and find that I can write these pages with it, it would be foolish on my part if I were seriously to entertain the idea that the object with which I was writing might not be really a pencil after all. For I have sufficient evidence that it is. Again, though I may conceivably be mistaken in seeing the text labelled *Phaedo* as a philosophical work, it would be foolish of me to entertain serious doubts about its being a philosophical work, if I proceed to read it and find that it contains a discussion of themes which are customarily described as philosophical.

We are back again with the idea of evidence. Sometimes the available evidence is such as to eliminate any reasonable doubt about the validity of an interpretation. If an object not only looks like a pencil but also functions as one, any further doubt about its being a pencil would be unreasonable. At other times the available evidence may not be sufficient to eliminate reasonable doubt. People still go on discussing whether the plays attributed to Shakespeare were actually written by him or by someone else. How precisely Aristotle's remarks in the third Book of the *De Anima* about the immortal intellect should be understood is still a matter of dispute. And, as has already been mentioned, there is room for different interpretations of Hegel's theory of the Absolute. Some interpretations could doubtless be excluded as incompatible with what Hegel plainly stated (an interpretation, for example, which turned Hegel into a materialist); but there is none the less more than one interpretation for which a plausible case can be made out. In fine, to claim that there are no data of experience which are completely free of interpretation is not to imply that all interpretations can properly be described as purely subjective constructions.

Perhaps the sceptic is trying to push us to the point at which we are driven to admit that internal coherence is the only criterion by which we can judge an historical account. What counts as evidence is, so to speak, part of the story. It is the historian who makes it evidence, who interprets it as such. We can legitimately expect or demand coherence and consistency, as in the case of a work of fiction. But we cannot get outside the account of the past and compare it with something which it is said to represent. For there is nothing with which to compare it.

In point of fact the situation is not like this. It is much more complex. It may well be the case that at some points historiography and historical fiction can resemble one another. They can do so, that is to say, unless we take a rather limiting view of the historian's role. For example, if someone writes an historical novel about Alexander the Great, he or she is likely to ascribe to Alexander certain thoughts, intentions or attitudes which are consistent with what is known of Alexander's character, life and actions. And if we are prepared to admit (as not everyone would be) that it is the part of the historian to reconstruct thoughts and intentions from actions, in this respect at least the historian can be said to resemble the writer of historical fiction. The fact remains however that in fiction as such evidence of the truth of the story is not required. If Conan Doyle were alive today and we seriously asked him for evidence that Sherlock Holmes wore a deerstalker's cap, this would show that we had mistaken the nature of the composition. It is indeed true that in a detective story evidence is mentioned and appealed to; but this evidence is clearly part of the story, an invention of the author. The historian does not invent his evidence, not at least in so far as he is an historian. Archives, archaeological discoveries and so on are not thought up or invented by the historian who relies on or appeals to them. And fresh evidence may show that his account or story has to be changed. To be sure, the historian has to see evidence as evidence. Otherwise he could not see it. But it no more follows that it is not evidence than it follows from the fact that I see an object as a pencil that it is not a pencil. It might perhaps be argued that 'evidence' is a relational term, and that nothing is evidence 'in itself'. Even so, if we say, for example, that certain archaeological discoveries constitute decisive evidence in support of a statement about an ancient civilization, we mean that the truth of the statement is the only reasonable explanation of what has been discovered. And if the statement will not fit into the story of the civilization as hitherto narrated, the story must be altered in such a way that it can incorporate the statement. Can *Alice in Wonderland* be affected in this way?

As for the history of philosophy, the sceptic might argue that though the story told by the historian must be compatible with his interpretations of the relevant texts, these interpretations are themselves part of the story. The criterion for judging the story is therefore simply internal coherence and consistency. The fact remains however that the historian is not free to interpret the texts just as he likes. Some statements may be ambiguous; but there are others, the meaning of which is clearly determined independently of the historian's will. For example, he is not at liberty to deny the fact that Marx asserted the priority of matter to spirit or mind. As far as the historian is concerned, the texts constitute something given, something which limits his reconstruction of the thought of philosophers. He no more invents them than the historian of England invents the relevant archives and records. And if his interpretation of records and texts are challenged, the proper procedure is to examine them again.

3. The lines of thought which have been briefly discussed in the preceding two sections of this chapter aimed at showing that historiography, by its very nature, cannot be objective, either because it treats of the non-existent, namely the past, or because it is impossible to make a clear distinction between datum and interpretation. We can now turn to the question whether the history of philosophy must not be permeated to some extent by subjectivity, on the ground that complete neutrality is a myth. It is not a question of history of philosophy being necessarily partisan in the ordinary sense. For it is

obvious that while an historian might write in such a way that his work would be an apologia for logical positivism or Marxism or Thomism or what not, he can also do his best to prescind from his own philosophical position or views and to be completely objective and neutral. Up to a point he can succeed in this attempt. That is to say, one history of philosophy can be less partisan or propagandistic than another. This is simply an empirical fact. It can be argued however that though one historian can be less partisan in his approach than another historian, it is not possible for him to attain complete neutrality or complete objectivity, however much he may try to do so. One historian may constantly intrude his own views, while another mentions them so little that the reader may be left wondering what they are. But it is still arguable that even the second historian cannot escape the influence of his own standpoint. For this inevitably expresses itself in, for example, the process of selection and choice of emphasis.

This line of thought found expression in the preface to the first volume of my *History of Philosophy*. I then maintained that the historian cannot write without some standpoint, 'if for no other reason than that he must have a principle of selection, guiding his intelligent choice and arrangement of facts'.[1] And I went on to state that the historian's 'own personal philosophical outlook is bound to influence his selection and presentation of facts or, at least, the emphasis which he lays on certain facts or aspects'.[2] This is the sort of topic which I wish to discuss briefly. Clearly, if someone writes a book about a particular philosopher or a particular movement or even about the development of philosophical thought in a certain culture or society or region, he is entitled, if he wishes, to select for treatment those themes or problems or aspects which interest him personally. He would be well advised to make it clear what he is doing, namely that his principle of selection is his personal interest and that he is not claiming to give an overall picture of, say, Plato's thought or of German idealism or of philosophy in India. But he is entitled to act in this way, provided that he does not claim to be doing something other than what he is actually doing. Here however we have a case of a deliberate policy, a policy of which the writer is fully aware and which he states. In the present context I am thinking not of a deliberate policy of this kind but rather of the question whether the historian's personal standpoint inevitably influences his writing, even if he does his best to eliminate such influence.

This question may perhaps seem rather far-fetched. But it is pretty obvious, for example, that unless an historian proposes to give an exhaustive catalogue of questions and opinions, a catalogue which would not normally be described as a history of philosophy, he has to pursue a policy of selection and he has to decide where the emphasis is to be placed. He need not of course deliberately select for emphasis those problems or those aspects of philosophy which most interest him personally. For he may try to place the emphasis where he believes that a given philosopher would place it, or where it would have been placed at the time or in the society of which he is treating. At the same time the inevitable process of selection and choice of emphasis implies the use of certain criteria. And the question at issue is whether the use made of certain criteria necessarily expresses the historian's personal philosophical standpoint, even if he is unaware of the fact. It might be argued, for example, that in his selection of problems and themes for treatment, or for more extended treatment, the historian is guided by his judgment about their relative importance, and that this judgment necessarily expresses a definite philosophical position.

The operative word in this contention is 'necessarily'. It hardly needs saying that if the historian selects for treatment, or at any rate for more extended treatment, those thinkers, problems, themes and movements which he personally, as a philosopher, considers important or really significant, his selection reveals something of his own philosophical position. Indeed, it amounts pretty well to a tautology to say that this is the case. For to say what philosophical problems one personally considers important is at any rate to give an indication of one's conception of the nature of philosophy. Though however it is possible for an historian to act in this way, it does not follow that it is necessary for him to do so. As has already been mentioned above, the historian might understand importance in terms of what the thinkers of whom he treats have considered important, and also in terms of influence. For instance, a given historian might consider a certain problem tiresome or even a pseudo-problem. But he might none the less try to show why X thought it important and devoted a lot of attention to it. The judgment that a given thinker attached great importance to certain problems or themes does not necessarily show that the historian regards them in the same way. By itself, the judgment reveals nothing about the historian's philosophical convictions. We can say the same in regard to a judgment about the influence of a given thinker. It can hardly be denied that Kant, for example, exercised a very considerable influence in a variety of ways. For this reason alone he could not be omitted from any history of Western philosophy. If therefore an historian judges that Kant's thought must be given a relatively extensive treatment, on the ground of its historical importance, this does not necessarily reveal anything of his personal attitude to Kant's philosophy.

The present writer therefore would not now wish to imply that every historian of philosophy has 'a principle of selection'[3] which reveals a philosophical point of view. For I doubt whether this is necessarily the case. As I have said elsewhere, 'the historian is not compelled to choose between summarizing conclusions and arranging the data to confirm a preconceived overall interpretative scheme . . . To put the matter in another way, the historian is not compelled to choose between superficiality on the one hand and propaganda for a certain system on the other. And it is misleading to suggest that he is so compelled'.[4] It is true that I was here thinking primarily of the activity of fitting the material to, say, Hegelian or Marxist presuppositions. But it seems to me that the quotation is relevant, if it is interpreted as also meaning that the historian is not compelled to choose between a purely doxographical approach on the one hand and estimating importance simply in terms of what is implied by his own philosophical position. For example, an historian might have little interest in philosophical theology. He might even think some at least of the problems in this area to be unanswerable and otiose. But he might none the less faithfully report the treatment of such problems by those who did consider them significant and important.

What should we say about the assertion that 'if the historian passes judgment on the philosophies of which he treats he will obviously do so from his own philosophical standpoint'?[5] We must, I think, make a distinction. An historian may indeed pass judgment on the theories of past philosophers from his own philosophical standpoint. He might see them, for example, in terms of Hegelian presuppositions. Suppose however that he confines himself to internal criticism, pointing out, for instance, what seem to him to be inconsistencies or incoherence or self-contradiction. In doing so he would be passing judgment. And in one sense, I suppose, he might be said to be expressing his own philosophical standpoint. For he would be using logical criteria which he personally accepted. At the same time, if he was using logical criteria which were accepted by his colleagues, it would be odd to say that he was judging philosophies in terms of his own philosophical standpoint. For 'his own' suggests something more personal than commonly accepted logical criteria. It suggests a point of view or position to which he adheres but which others may not share.

What I have been saying should not be taken as implying that in my opinion an historian's personal philosophical standpoint does not in practice influence his writing in some way or other. It is possible, I suppose, to write a textbook of philosophy in which selection and emphasis are decided by purely conventional or utilitarian standards.[6] But if the historian really enters into discussion of themes, it is unlikely that no trace of his personal standpoint will be discernible. At the same time if selection and emphasis are determined, for example, by the criterion of importance, this criterion can, as I have argued, be understood in more than one way. In a treatment of St Thomas Aquinas, for instance, it may be understood as referring to what Aquinas himself thought important. And in this case I do not think that the principle of selection and emphasis necessarily expresses the historian's own philosophical standpoint.

4. It may be said that in the foregoing remarks I have passed over in silence an important relevant factor, relevant, that is to say, to the objectivity of historical writing. Hegel asserted that no philosophy can transcend 'its contemporary world'.[7] And if this statement is accepted, cannot it be applied to the history of philosophy? The historian's reconstruction of the past is a reconstruction in the present; and is not this reconstruction inevitably influenced by the outlook of the society to which the historian belongs, by what Hegel called the *Zeitgeist*, the spirit of the time, by its way of thinking, its ideas, its language and so on? The historian of philosophy does not exist in a vacuum. He lives in a concrete historical situation, in a definite cultural milieu. He has been initiated into its speech and ways of thought,

its standards and ideals. He has become a participant in common perspectives. And he cannot escape its influence. Even if he reacts against some contemporary ideas or standards or ways of thinking, his revolt is none the less conditioned by his milieu or situation. And does not this affect his reconstruction of the past and exclude complete objectivity?

A preliminary comment on the line of thought expressed in the first paragraph of this section is that it is extremely vague. What, for example, is meant by the claim that the historian of philosophy cannot transcend his time? If it were interpreted as meaning that the historian cannot foresee the future, it could be accepted without any difficulty. For even if someone believes that the course of history is determined and that future events are foreseeable in principle, he will presumably admit that in view of the vast number of factors involved nobody, including the historian, can in practice foresee the future, not at least in the sense intended.[8] It by no means follows however that an historian's inability to foresee the future affects the objectivity of his reconstruction of the past. If an historian of Russia is unable to foresee the future of the Soviet Union, this does not affect the objectivity of his account of the 1917 revolution. And if an historian of philosophy is unable to foretell (conjecture apart) the future course of philosophy, this does not affect his reconstruction of the historical development of philosophical thought up to date. In any case the historian is by definition concerned with the past. His ability or inability to foresee the future is therefore irrelevant to his task as an historian.

Again, if it is said that the historian of philosophy sees the past from the perspective of the present, of contemporary society for example, what precisely is meant by 'contemporary society'? And how precisely are the ways of thought of contemporary society supposed to influence, or perhaps even determine, the historian's reconstruction of the past?

Such requests for precise statement may seem to constitute an evasive policy, an attempt, that is to say, to evade a real problem by demanding an exactitude or precision which it is very difficult, if indeed possible, to provide. So we had better admit that people, including historians, are influenced by the ways of thought of their cultural milieu. How indeed could it be otherwise? We can indeed revolt against ideas and standards and values which we have been taught in the process of education, in the process of initiation into the society to which we belong. But a reasoned opposition will doubtless be expressed in terms which we believe to be intelligible by the 'contemporary mind', or at least by the sort of people whom we are addressing. If I am born and live in twentieth-century England, it hardly needs saying that I do not think and react like a contemporary of Confucius in ancient China. To be sure, there may be, and in my opinion are, some constants in human nature (otherwise we would not speak of 'man'), but it would be idle to deny that there are differences between, say, an educated American of today and a Red Indian of days gone by. Given sufficient reflection, we could doubtless specify some differences in ways of thought and reaction.

The very fact however that we can discuss and suggest such differences in ways of thought shows that we are not so determined by the characteristics of our cultural milieu that we are unable to enter into the mentalities of people belonging to other societies. A contemporary American may look at world problems from a perspective which is different from that of a Soviet citizen. But it by no means follows that the American is debarred in principle from understanding the outlook of the Soviet citizen. He may not share it. But this is irrelevant to the point at issue. A given modern historian of philosophy may not share the theistic world-view of the leading medieval philosophers; but this does not necessarily prevent him from understanding their outlook and giving a fair account of it. It is all very well to talk about the autonomy of different language-games. If I can present an intelligible case for the contention that members of a past society played a certain language-game which expressed a way of life in which I do not participate, I must be able to understand this outlook and this language-game, unless indeed one so defines 'understanding' that it becomes true by definition that I do not understand them.[9] It might indeed be objected that in the case of a past society I cannot prove that I have understood its way of thinking. But then it cannot be proved that I do not understand it. For both procedures would involve appeal to relevant evidence, records, writings and so on. In point of fact the burden of proof rests on the shoulders of anyone who maintains that a twentieth-century European historian of philosophy is unable to enter into the mind of Plato or Aristotle or Plotinus or Confucius or Samkhara

In some cases this penetration is more difficult than in others. But the reasons why this is so are specifiable. And there seems to me no good reason why an historian of philosophy should be unable in principle to obtain some real understanding of, say, ancient Chinese or Japanese thought.

It is still open to anyone to insist that, despite all attempts at understanding the outlooks and ways of thought of past centuries, the twentieth-century European or American historian of philosophy will none the less look at the past from a twentieth-century perspective, and that he cannot get away from it. I suspect however that in the long run this means little more than that a man who is born and lives in twentieth-century Europe or America cannot live in any other century. This is true but trivial. If anything more than this is meant, it must be that the historian in question is influenced in his reconstruction of the past by ways of thought characteristic of his own time and of the society to which he belongs. Though however this influence is undoubtedly strong in the first instance, it seems to me obvious that this constricting or restrictive influence can be progressively overcome, and that the outstanding historian is one who, among other qualifications, shows his ability to enter into and clarify past mentalities, outlooks and attitudes. If 'complete objectivity' is interpreted as involving a supra-historical position, a position outside time, it is unobtainable. And if it is unobtainable, as it obviously is, it is foolish to take the position in question as a standard for judging objectivity. We have to employ standards which are of practical use in determining degrees of objectivity. And there are such standards.

A final point. The historian of philosophy is concerned with the historical development of philosophical thought. It may be difficult, as we have already noted, to determine precisely what is and what is not to be recognized as philosophical thought. But the historian is certainly not compelled to use a narrow criterion determined, for example, by what, in his own philosophical circle, is considered to be 'scientific' philosophy. At the same time there are some limits to what can reasonably be described as philosophy. And it is obviously easier to understand outlooks and attitudes which have been expressed in philosophical reflection than it is to understand the mentalities of societies that had nothing which could reasonably be described as philosophy. The philosophy of the past is not impenetrable by the philosopher of the present day. And if anyone suggests that past philosophy, as reconstructed or rethought by the historian, is nothing more than the philosophy of the present projected into the past, the burden of proof rests on his shoulders. So far however from his being able to prove it, I doubt whether he can even make out a reasonable case for his thesis. He is likely to appeal to a criterion of objectivity which, by the nature of the case, is unusable.

Notes

[1] *A History of Philosophy*, Vol. 1, p. v.
[2] *Ibid.*
[3] *A History of Philosophy*, Vol. 1, p. v.
[4] *The Heythrop Journal*, Vol. XIV (April, 1973), p. 134. This article represents my inaugural lecture in the University of London. It is reprinted in *Philosophers and Philosophies* (London, 1976). The quotation appears on p. 27.
[5] *Ibid.*
[6] If the writer's intention is simply to•help students to pass examinations, and if selection and emphasis are determined simply by what he believes that examiners are likely to expect, I would describe this as a utilitarian consideration. But I do so with apologies to the utilitarian philosopher.
[7] *Sämtliche Werke* (ed. H. Glochner, Stuttgart, 1928-56), VII, p. 35.
[8] We can obviously make conjectures about the future course of events. And in the case of fairly simple causal relations we can foretell the future with a high degree of probability. For example, if we know that someone is now eating a deadly poison, for which there is no known antidote, we can foretell that he will soon die. But when we talk about inability to foresee the future, we are not normally referring to this kind of case.
[9] If 'understanding' were so defined as to entail the conclusion that no idea or outlook or attitude could be understood unless it was shared, it would then be true by definition that I could not understand an idea or outlook which I did not share. But to make one's thesis true by definition in this way would be a poor sort of argument.

CHAPTER III

ETHICS AND METAPHYSICS: EAST AND WEST

For understandable reasons the reputation of St Thomas Aquinas has undergone a certain slump in recent years. There seem, however, to be signs of a reversal of this trend. For one thing it may have become better understood how the achievements of St Thomas in the cultural situation of western medieval Christendom can provide a source of inspiration and stimulus for those who are faced with a fragmented world which, none the less, aspires after a unity transcending and yet subsuming in itself cultural differences. It is not a question of returning to the Middle Ages, which one could not do, even should one so desire. Nor is it a question of achieving a definitive synthesis, fixed and immutable for all time. To bring together, however, into a unified vision of reality, a unified interpretation of the world, man and human history, the various branches of human knowledge, and the various aspects of human life and experience, remains a valid ideal. The thoughts of St Thomas remind us of this ideal and spur us on to make some modest contribution to its realization which, by the nature of the case, can never be complete.[1]

In our search for unity, dialogue between East and West appears to be a factor of great importance; I have chosen, therefore, the subject, 'Ethics and Metaphysics: East and West.' Though my very limited acquaintance with eastern thought may make this presumptuous, it may be excused by the conviction that East and West have something to offer one another. Here, it will be possible to suggest but a few lines of thought relevant to the theme.

Ethics or moral philosophy is obviously concerned with the human agent, the person, and his conduct. In teleological ethics, in which the concept of the good is primary, the end to be attained, however conceived, is attained through human action. In deontological ethics, in which the concepts of obligation and duty are primary, obligation bears on the human will. It is simply a truism to say that the human being and his conduct are central to ethics; and this applies to eastern as well as to western philosophy. When, in the *Gītā*, Krishna speaks to Arjuna about the need for disinterested, rather than self-cen-

66

tred and self-seeking, action, he is obviously referring to the way in which human beings ought to act, not to what Brahman or the Absolute ought to do. Again, when a Buddhist enunciates the eightfold path, right motive, right speech, right conduct and so on, he has in mind the individual human agent. Confucian ethics, too, is obviously concerned with man in his social relations, as a member of this or that social *nexus*.

If, however, one prescinds for the moment from certain developments in post-medieval western philosophy, it is clear that ethics or moral philosophy has generally formed part of an overall interpretation of reality. In western thought this is obviously true of Aristotle, the Stoics and Neoplatonism in the ancient world; of medieval theologians and philosophers, such as Aquinas; and, in later times, of Spinoza, the German idealists, such as Fichte and Hegel, of F.H. Bradley in England and Royce in America. In the East the link between ethics and metaphysics has been exemplified in the Vedic schools of India, in Buddhist thought,[2] in Taoism, and in the illuminationist and Sufi traditions of the Islamic world. I do not wish to discuss here the question of the logical relation between judgments of value and metaphysical or theological propositions which purport to be factual assertions about reality; that is, the 'no-*ought*-from-an-*is*' thesis. Whether it be valid or invalid, it remains true that ethics has commonly formed part of a general philosophical outlook of some kind or other. The point which I wish to make here is the rather obvious one that our general philosophical outlook, our metaphysics if you like, can powerfully influence our view of the human person and of the status of ethics and moral distinctions. To be sure, when it is a question of what influences what and when, there is room for endless discussion from which, however, I must prescind.

Needless to say, we cannot equate western philosophy with pluralism and eastern thought with monism.[3] Firstly, there have been monist philosophies in the West, from Parmenides through Spinoza and on to F. H. Bradley. Secondly, eastern philosophy cannot be equated simply with Indian thought, nor is Indian thought identifiable with monism. The Cārrāka philosophy was not monistic, nor was the Nyāya-Vaiśesika system among the Vedic schools. Obviously, too, the Vedānta philosophy cannot be equated to the monism of Śamkhara. For example, the Advaita system of Śamkhara gave rise to a reaction, as can be seen in the theistic system of Madhva. At the same time, it seems true to say that what has tended to prevail in western thought has been pluralism, while in Hindu philosophy it has been monism, or at least, the idea of the all-comprehending One. Martin Heidegger maintained that western philosophy in concentrating on beings had forgotten Being; and there seems to be some truth in this contention. In any case, I am considering pluralism and monism here as two types of philosophy, both of which are represented in the East and the West, but of which pluralism is more representative of the West and monism more representative of Indian thought, at least of the Vedānta philosophy.

Let us assume, first of all, that the pluralistic world of ordinary experience and of science is real. This world includes persons, each of whom is a dynamic centre of energy and correlative, in a sense, to his or her own world, though it also makes sense to speak of a common world, a world of multiplicity. Since, however, human persons are not simply isolated atoms, but live in societies of various kinds, problems relating to moral standards, standards of conduct, inevitably arise. Reflection on these problems gives birth to moral philosophy. Whether the emphasis is placed on the development of the individual's potentialities or on social relations and obligations, the bedrock reality of ethics inevitably consists of the plurality of persons, of selves. The basic datum of ethics will be the plurality of persons living in a common world. In a pluralistic philosophy there is no question of regarding personality or individual selfhood as something to be overcome though, to be sure, *anarchic* individualism, unbridled egoism, will have to be subdued if there is to be any moral order at all. The moral order to be constructed and preserved within the existing natural order may be conceived as a unity-in-multiplicity, a 'kingdom of ends' to use a Kantian phrase; but the multiplicity will be an essential element. What is envisaged is a society of persons realizing shared ideals through action; in other words, the individual personality or selfhood is regarded as a morally inviolable value.

A positive evaluation of personality or selfhood will be intensified or reinforced if the ultimate reality, the source of the empirical world, is conceived as being itself personal. Finite personality would then appear, not as something to be negated, but as a limited reflection of divine personality. Further, man is likely to look on himself as having a divine vocation to contribute, by what he makes of himself and by his actions in the world, to the realization of a divinely determined end or goal of human life and history. This is true of all theistic religions, Jewish, Christian or Muslim. We may add, however, that if the divine personality is conceived, not simply in terms of one Person, but in Trinitarian terms, this belief should intensify the ideal of a unified human society, a society of persons, as the goal of history. In fine, theistic religion or theistic metaphysics seems to entail a positive evaluation of human personality or selfhood. Immortality or resurrection, for example, are conceived as personal immortality and as the resurrection of the human person.

In such a philosophical outlook where personality is taken as a category which applies even to the divine reality, great emphasis is likely to be placed on ethics, on the moral development of the human person and on goal-directed ideas in this world. Ethics can, of course, become detached from any theological background. If a pluralistic philosophy or world-view is retained, however, even more weight may be placed upon human action, inasmuch as the construction of a moral world-order within the natural order is then seen as dependent not on God, but on man alone. This can be seen in both secular humanism and in Marxism.

Suppose, however, that the empirical world, which for the pluralist is a real world, though not necessarily coterminous with all reality, is believed to be in some sense illusory. That is, suppose that the empirical world is only the appearance of one single reality, the Absolute, and that this appearance is the fruit of ignorance, of the mind's limitations. Individual personality or selfhood will also appear as illusory, as something to be overcome or transcended through the finite spirit's realization of its oneness with the sole reality, the infinite Spirit or Absolute. While ethics will not indeed be abolished or discarded, moral purification will be regarded as a condition for and a step on the way to transcending the finite ego or self. This means that, though ethics will of course include a theory of conduct, of action, the emphasis will be placed not so much on social action as on enlightenment, on progress in realization of the truth about reality. Thus, for the Vedānta monist the oneness of the finite spirit in its inmost essence — in what Meister Eckhart called the 'spark' or 'citadel' of the soul — with infinite Spirit is an already existing ontological fact, though it is obscured by ignorance. For the Buddhist thinker enlightenment involves seeing through the illusory character of the concept of the permanent self, including the Hindu concept of *atman*. In other words, ethics is geared to enlightenment and to liberation from the self or ego. In this sense it is oriented away from the empirical world of multiplicity, of a plurality of things and persons, which, for the pluralist, is a real world even though not necessarily coextensive with all reality.

There is a further point to note. In any monist system ethical distinctions between good and bad, right and wrong, are likely to be regarded as relative to the limited human point of view. Such distinctions are transcended in the Absolute. Ethics, so to speak, is not supreme, and with the disappearance of the ego, ethics disappears too.

To avoid misunderstanding, I wish to repeat that I am not proposing a simple identification of western thought with pluralism, with emphasis on the value of the human person and with a dynamic social ethics. Nor am I proposing an identification of eastern thought with monism, with a view of the self as unreal and as to be transcended, and with an ethics geared to union with the Absolute or, in the case of Buddhism, to the attainment of Nirvāna. If we consider my suggestion that in any monist system emphasis is likely to be placed on the process of enlightenment and that ethical distinctions will be regarded as relative to the human point of view, we can recognize that such features of monist thought are not confined to the East but are exemplified in, for example, the philosophies of Spinoza and Bradley. As for eastern thought, what has been said hardly applies to Confucianism, for example, which is pre-eminently a social ethics. Moreover, both Hinduism and Buddhism are so complex that anything said about either is likely to be open to criticism or challenge. In Hindu philosophy there have been pluralist systems. In certain forms of Buddhism enlightenment does not involve "leaving" the empirical world, but seeing that the Absolute and phenomenal reality are one and the same. The empirical world may be seen differently after enlightenment; nevertheless, the ideal will be, not that of mystical absorption in a transcendent reality, but enlightened action in the only world there is.

At the same time, it seems true to say that the general direction of western thought has been towards pluralism and anthropocentric thinking. Even the so-called linguistic philosophy can be described as anthropocentric, in the sense that it is concerned with a specifically human phenomenon. Further, the West has developed social ethics and social philosophy: the revolt against the aridities of meta-ethics has been, not so much a demand for the incorporation of ethics in a metaphysical or a theological framework, as a demand that philosophers should concern themselves with relevant and substantive social and moral issues. In contrast and generally speaking, classical Indian philosophy has been one of liberation, centred upon the relationship of the finite spirit to the ultimate reality and aiming at enlightment of a religious type. To be sure, there are Indian philosophers today who pay scant attention to classical Indian philosophy and who have adopted such western ways of thought as logical or conceptual analysis. But I have been speaking of the native tradition of Indian thought, not of the importation of western philosophy.

If it were to be claimed that western thought has been anthropocentric, whereas philosophy in India is centred upon the Absolute, the assertion would clearly be open to criticism. Let us leave the West aside. It might be maintained that in the course of its development Indian philosophy has become increasingly anthropocentric. This may sound paradoxical. But if the Absolute or Brahman is beyond all conceptualization, as the Upanishads teach,[4] there is little to be said about it, except that it is invisible, inaudible, intangible, unimaginable, and transcending human thought. What can be referred to is man's relationship to the ultimate reality and the ways of approaching truth and union. In this sense the philosophy of the Vedānta might be described as anthropocentric, however odd the description may sound, for after all it is concerned with human liberation and salvation. The same might be said of the Sufi philosophy as represented, for example, by Suhrawardi in the twelfth century and by Shirazi (or Mulla Sadrā) in the seventeenth century. The Sufi thinkers developed a metaphysics in which God was described as Existence itself, the ocean of Being to which finite things were related in a manner analogous to that of the waves to the sea. But it is not unreasonable to regard their chief interest as being the illumination and 'ascent' to God of the finite spirit.

In sum, in western thought since the Middle Ages there has been a marked tendency to separate ethics from any explicit metaphysical or theological framework or background.[5] It has tended to represent man as a this-worldly being, without any real relation to a transcendent divine reality. This is clear in naturalism, for example, in secular humanism, in Marxism, in the existentialism of Sartre, and in positivism. The indigenous thought of India, however, as also that of the illuminationist and Sufi traditions in Islam, emphasizes man's relationship to a reality transcending the phenomenal world. It is all very well to say that Indian preoccupation with the Absolute and man's relationship to it stands, or has stood, in the way of a dynamic concern with social progress and with action directed to the common good. Probably there is some truth in this. Some Indians today are inclined to think that 'religion is the curse of India'.

The question arises however whether man is a purely this-worldly being. May not Hindu philosophy be correct in maintaining that the finite spirit is oriented to infinite spirit? Were not such philosophers in the West as Bergson, Karl Jaspers and Gabriel Marcel justified in reacting against naturalism, positivism, and purely secular humanism? In other words, the question of the nature of man can arise with urgency out of a confrontation of East and West. If man is indeed open to a transcendent reality, the task is surely that of trying to harmonize the dynamism of the West with the truth contained in the religious traditions of India and of Islam. This need has been felt by an Indian philosopher such as Sri Aurobindo and, in the West, by Teilhard de Chardin. Both groups might gain by frank discussion about the nature of man and that to which he is open. At the same time, it seems to me that reflection on man, his conduct, and his vocation cannot be profitably pursued if metaphysics is excluded.

This last contention can be illustrated in the following way. In one main stream of western thought moral philosophy has tended to take the form of meta-ethics, in the sense of an examination of the language of morals. While it is not possible to discuss here the reasons for this development, it should be asked how the language of morals can be understood, unless it be seen as a human activity, as expressing a form of life, to use a Wittgensteinian phrase. I do not think that it can. All distinguishable language-games are human activities, rooted in the complex nature of man. In the long run, therefore, does not a philosophical inquiry into language, as a human phenomenon, demand a theory of man, a philosophical anthropology? What is more, man is not an isolated entity, existing in a void. He is a being in the world; and any adequate philosophy of man demands an overall view of man and his environment, that is, some manner of world-view. We are, then, led on to questions about the nature of reality, and here there is ample opportunity for dialogue between East and West.

Here, the word 'dialogue' means, of course, creative dialogue between thinkers who are concerned only with the pursuit of truth and who are open to other points of view. Certainly, numerous western philosophers have dismissed the philosophies of the East either as religious mysticism or as unsystematic moralizing which does not really deserve the name of philosophy as we understand it. Some eastern thinkers have turned their backs on the philosophical traditions of their countries to embrace one or another line of western thought, such as analysis, phenomenology, or Marxism. These points of view express a lamentable prejudice and bias which, while understandable, are no less regrettable. There is truth in Martin Heidegger's contention that the West has forgotten Being, and it may well be that the East is in imminent danger of doing the same. Philosophers of both East and West might well start, as did Heidegger, with reflection on man himself, the questioner. This is perhaps the core of my message.

The impression which Indian thought makes on most westerners is obviously one of other-worldliness. That is to say, we tend to think of Indian philosophy as religiously-oriented thought, geared to liberation and to union with the One, however this may be conceived in this or that system. Ethics is certainly present, but it forms a phase of a movement which transcends the narrow confines of the ego and indeed of the phenomenal world in general. Much the same can be said of the illuminist and Sufi traditions in Islam and, in the West of, for example, the philosophy of Plotinus. When we turn to China and Japan, however, we find a rather different atmosphere. It is true that we can find the search for enlightenment, as in Zen Buddhism, and the other-worldliness of Pure Land Buddhism with its emphasis on the saving grace of the Amitabha Buddha.

For the most part, however, the emphasis is more on life in this world and, in particular on social relations. This is obviously true in the case of Confucianism, which became the official ideology of imperial China. Some writers assert that whereas in western thought man has been conceived primarily in terms of the individual, in the East, meaning, above all, China and Japan, man has been conceived primarily in terms of his social relations.

Hearing a sweeping statement of this kind, objections tend to spring up in our minds. With regard to the West, we may refer, for example, to Plato's and Aristotle's conceptions of man as a member of the polis; to the medieval writers' preoccupation with social and political themes and the relations between large-scale societies, such as the church and the feudal state; to Hegel's emphasis on man's participation in the we-consciousness, in the self-consciousness of a greater whole; and to Marxism, which, though a philosophy of western origin, defines man in terms of his social relations. On the other hand, with regard to China, we may point out that in Taoism there was less emphasis on social relations than in Confucianism, and that in Buddhist thought stress was laid on the individual working out his own salvation within of course the conditions set by the effects of one's past good and bad actions.

While the general statement in question does need qualification, it may nonetheless be true that in the West: 1) we have come to think, with approval, of the emergence of the individual from the background of a closely-knit society, such as the tribe; 2) we have tended to lay increasing emphasis on the value of the person and on the individual's development, and 3) we now think in terms of a pluralistic society and of the individual's right to his own judgment in the ethical, religious and political sphere, provided he does not infringe the rights of others. To be sure, there have been and are collectivist and totalitarian systems of thought, but they evoke strong reactions, and it seems evident that totalitarianism is maintained only by means of coercion and repression.

As for China, it is perhaps significant that it was neither Taoism nor Buddhism but Confucianism, a system of social ethics,[6] which became the official ideology of imperial China. It is obviously possible to give an historical account of the victory of Communism in modern China, in which little, if any, reference is made to philosophical ideas about man. Nevertheless, it is arguable that Marxism, as interpreted by the late Chairman Mao, has found real points of insertion in Chinese ways of thought, despite the fact that in some important respects it runs counter to ancient Chinese tradition.

In Japan the situation is obviously different. Nevertheless, Japanese scholars themselves have drawn attention to the way in which man has always been conceived as a member of a group.[7] Though it is possible that individualism may be making some headway expressions of this traditional way of thinking are to be found even in industrialized Japan.[8] Doubtless, in one way or another the ideas of universal and particular find expression in both East and West. Yet it by no means follows that there is no difference in the placement of emphases.

However this may be, both ways of thinking contain truth and need harmonization. Man obviously is a social being; Aristotle's famous statement remains as true now as it ever was, namely, that he who stands in no need of society is either a beast or a god, either infrahuman or suprahuman.[9] Though ethics is not reducible to social ethics, Hegel seems to have been quite justified in emphasizing the specification of concrete duties and obligations in terms of social relations. It is not simply a question of duties being specified by one's membership in a given existing social nexus, such as the family or the state, for the attempt to realize shared ideal values is a social task. One of our most pressing ethical tasks is the progressive realization of a unified and harmonious world-society, one which while respecting cultural differences, will transcend the limits set by national boundaries. In Hegelian terms, an identity-in-difference seems the goal. From the metaphysical point of view this unity of human persons would reflect the unity of the infinite Spirit, the creative energy in the process of evolution. The natural order provides the context, so to speak, within which the unified moral order should be progressively constructed.

At the same time, the human person possesses an intrinsic value. Man is not entirely definable in terms of his social relations. In the West, the value of the human person was secured, in theory at least, by Christian theology. Hegel may well have been right when he maintained that what he called 'the principle of subjectivity' was introduced into the world by Christianity. He was also probably right in maintaining that for a long time the principle was realized only, or at any rate mainly, on the plane of interiority and that only through a long historical process has it come to find expression in the sphere of social and political structures. The question arises, however, whether full recognition of the value and freedom of the individual, the human person, can be maintained if the human being's relationship to the transcendent is denied or lost sight of, if, that is to say, man is conceived as a purely this-worldly being as in Marxism. Some would claim that it can; in their opinion, a judgment of value about human personality can be detached from any metaphysical or theological anchorage. So it can, in the sense that the judgment can be made even by someone who rejects the metaphysical or theological beliefs with which it was once associated. If, however, man is regarded as a purely this-wordly being, the value of the individual is likely to be estimated in terms of his social contribution. Both East and West are threatened by this reduction of man to a purely this-worldly being. He is, of course, a being in the world; but is he only this, or is the human spirit oriented to Infinite Spirit, as has been held, in their several ways by Christian, Hindu and Islamic thinkers?

Let me express my point in this way. Henri Bergson argued that the world was becoming unified on the plane of science and technology, that one body was being formed. This body, however, needed the infusion of a soul, and for Bergson this need could be met only through an infusion of mystical religion through contact with the divine Spirit. I have great sympathy with Bergson's point of view. Apart, however, from the fact that mysticism cannot be manufactured at will, the question arises whether mystical religion does not turn man's attention away from tasks in this world, from the active realization of shared ethical ideals through action in history. This is a question to which Bergson himself gave some thought. It has also attracted the attention of others, such as Sri Aurobindo, who wished to show that Indian philosophical and religious thought could be true to itself while at the same time undergoing reinterpretation in a way that would admit of western dynamism and emphasis on work in this world. This theme is well-suited for dialogue between East and West.

Some in the West look to the East for wisdom, for illumination about the meaning of life, and for a view of the nature of reality which goes beyond the picture of the world painted by the empirical sciences. Assuming that the religious beliefs and philosophical systems of the West are played out or bankrupt, they turn instead to the Vedānta, Zen Buddhism, and so on. This assumption does not appear well-founded. Besides, it can be argued that the East, if by this we mean their traditional religious and philosophical beliefs, has also proved bankrupt, in the sense that it has failed to provide the basis for the dynamic social policies demanded by the modern world, and that the western philosophy has occupied this vacant space. At the same time one can sympathize with those who turn away from what they regard, rightly or wrongly, as the operative ideals of modern western society and who find the values for which they are looking in eastern ways of thought. That such people are sometimes rather naive and fall victim to charlatans posing as revealers of esoteric wisdom is irrelevant to the fact that, to a number of people, the religious and philosophical traditions of eastern origin appear to present a challenge to western society and its operative, as opposed to its professed, ideals. That there is such a challenge can be felt even by people who remain sincerely attached to the Christian religion, but who are convinced of the need for a real, living and constructive dialogue.[10]

It is obviously impossible to discuss here in an adequate manner this challenge presented by the East. One suggestion, however, may serve to pull together the threads of this address.

In the ancient world, especially in the Hellenistic epoch, such philosophies as, for example, Stoicism and Neoplatonism, tended to be, or to offer, a way of life incorporated into a general view of reality. In the Middle Ages people looked to the Christian religion for a way of life or path to salvation, rather than to philosophy as distinct from what St Thomas called 'sacred doctrine'. In St Augustine's use of the term 'philosophy', Christianity was itself the true philosophy. With thinkers such as St Thomas, however, philosophical ethics formed part of a total Christian worldview. In the post-medieval world there has been a progressive separation of moral philosophy from theological and metaphysical presuppositions. Ethics has been declared autonomous; this declaration of independence has been justified, theoretically by the 'no-*ought*-from-an-*is*' thesis. We have further seen the reduction of moral philosophy to meta-ethics, discussion of substantive issues being left to preachers, 'moralists' and others, though, as noted, there has been a reaction against this very limited idea of the function of moral philosophy.

In the eastern traditions, however, philosophy continued to offer a way of life, a path to liberation; there, ethics has been part of a general view of reality and of man's relationship to reality. We can see this not only in the philosophy of the Vedánta, in Buddhist thought and in Sufism, but also in Taoism and even to some extent in Confucianism, with its somewhat vague references to T'ien or Heaven. It is perfectly understandable that some people, therefore, find in eastern thought what to them seems to be missing in modern western philosophy — to be, indeed, conspicuous by its absence. No doubt one of the attractions of Buddhism, especially Zen Buddhism, for some minds is that it does not commit them to beliefs about what Kant called 'super-sensible reality', beliefs which are found in theistic religion and which they feel unable to accept. Such considerations do not appear, however, to constitute a complete explanation of the attraction of eastern thought which offers ways of life and paths to liberation and salvation, with various degrees of metaphysical support.

It may be said that the very developments in western thought which alienate some minds constitute a genuine advance in philosophical thinking, and that the classical eastern philosophies are doomed to extinction by the spreading enlightenment from the West. But it is here that there arises a challenge to western philosophy to rethink its conception of moral philosophy and of its relation to a general view of reality. I have argued that ethics demands or leads to a philosophical anthropology, and that this, in turn, leads to a metaphysics or reality. It is not required that we should simply accept one or another eastern philosophy, as though it were the sole repository of wisdom. But eastern thought can serve as a reminder and a challenge to a process of constructive thought which could fill a vacuum and serve as a basis for the development of a worldwide moral order and a truly human society.

Notes

[1] For example, human knowledge develops and grows. Man's scientific knowledge, for instance, is now far greater than in the thirteenth century, but there is no good reason to suppose that it will remain as it is now.

[2] It may be objected that Buddhism, at least Theravada Buddhism, evades metaphysics. This is true up to a point. At the same time it would appear that Buddhist phenomenalistic analysis of empirical reality, including the self, may be regarded as metaphysics. Further, even if Nirvāna is to be conceived as a state rather than an entity, it is certainly not equivalent to nothingness in the ordinary sense.

[3] By monism in this context, I understand 'substantial' rather than 'attributive', monism.

[4] The sacred texts do not represent only one uniform way of speaking. But an insistence on the divine reality as being 'above reasoning', as the Katha Upanishad states, is a prominent feature of the Upanishads and so of the Vedánta philosophy.

[5] I include the word 'explicit' in order to allow for the fact that an implicit metaphysics or ontology can be present, even when metaphysics is explicitly rejected. Often we encounter the implicit assumption that, in principle, 'to be' is to be a possible object of sense-experience. To my mind this assumption constitutes an implicit ontology or metaphysics.

[6] In Neo-Confucianism there was indeed a good deal of metaphysical or cosmological speculation. But it was as a system of social ethics that Confucianism was raised to the status of an official ideology, an instrument of education for those in public service.

[7] Cf. Hajime Nakamura, *Ways of Thinking of Eastern Peoples*, revised English translation edited by Philip P. Wiener (Honolulu, 1964).

[8] For example, the factory is conceived more as an extended family or social group than as a mere collection of isolated individuals who happen to spend their working hours in the same place.

[9] Aristotle was indeed referring to the *polis*, but to refuse to give the statement a wider connotation would be pedantic. Aristotle thought in terms of the Greek *polis*, Hegel in terms of the national state. The time is coming, or has come, when we should be thinking in terms of one human society.

[10] E.G. Dom Bede Griffiths, who has for some years been living in an ashram in India.

CHAPTER IV

SOME ASPECTS OF MEDIEVAL PHILOSOPHY

1. In the early Middle Ages philosophy amounted to little more than logic or dialectic, which was classified as one of the liberal arts. This statement stands in need of qualification of course. For example, it was in the ninth century that John Scotus Erigena developed his speculative system, based on the Neoplatonist tradition and Patristic thought. By and large however philosophy tended to be identified with logic. And this helps to explain the concept of philosophy as the handmaid of theology. Aristotle at any rate regarded logic as a propaedeutic to and as an instrument for the development of the sciences. In the Middle Ages theology was regarded as the chief science. As long therefore as philosophy amounted to little more than logic, it was conceived as the instrument, or handmaid, of theology. At least it was so regarded by the theologians, especially when the dialecticians busied themselves with substantial issues which were thought to be no concern of theirs.

With increasing knowledge of the thought of the Greco-Roman world, and also of the Islamic culture, the concept of philosophy naturally broadened. And, as with Aristotle, the word 'philosophy' came to include most branches of study apart from history (in the sense of chronicles) and medicine. It is of course misleading to say that physics, astronomy and economics were included in philosophy. For these terms naturally bring to mind sciences which have developed since the Middle Ages. We can say however that study of material things as subject to motion, of the heavenly bodies and of the relations between types of society fell under the general heading of philosophy, whether theoretical philosophy, as in the case of physics, or practical philosophy, as in the case of ethics and political theory. Mathematics belonged to theoretical philosophy.

In other words, philosophy comprised the greater part of secular knowledge or what was thought to be such. And this fact helps to explain the prominence of philosophical studies in the medieval academic curriculum. One first acquired secular knowledge and then went on to acquire what was thought to be revealed knowledge or knowledge derived from revealed

80

premises.

Philosophy in this wide sense obviously possessed a certain measure of autonomy. For it was regarded as treating of substantial issues which fell within its own province, and not simply as an instrument to be applied in a science other than itself. At the same time it was closely related to theology in a variety of ways.

The most obvious relationship was an extrinsic one. That is to say, it was assumed that there were certain truths revealed by God or implied by revealed truths; and if a philosopher pursued a line of thought or made assertions which were thought to be incompatible with revelation, he was called to order by the ecclesiastical authorities. It was not however simply a case of individual propositions, which were thought to be erroneous on theological grounds. It is evident that in the thirteenth century the conservative theologians and the ecclesiastical authorities formed the impression that a naturalistic world-view was being presented or at any rate insinuated by the philosophers of the Faculty of Arts, and by some theologians too. Hence the condemnation in 1277 of a long list of assorted propositions, a condemnation which really represented a strong reaction on the part of conservative elements against what they regarded as a growing tendency to naturalism.

Objections to philosophical speculation on theological grounds were not confined to medieval Christendom. They were raised, for example, in the Moslem world in Southern Spain. And they also occurred in Judaism, though here objections tended to centre upon attitudes towards the Law rather than upon doctrinal matters.

It would however be a mistake to conceive the relation between philosophy and theology in the MiddleAges as a purely external one, in the sense that theologians and philosophers were two distinct groups, the first of which restricted the freedom of thought of the latter. The academic career culminated in occupation of a chair of theology, and most of the leading philosophers of the Middle Ages were theologians, such as Bonaventure, Aquinas, Giles of Rome, Duns Scotus and Ockham. There were indeed philosophers in the Faculty of Arts, but they tended to stick to exposition, especially of Aristotle. It must be added that they were encouraged to do so. Indeed, at Paris they were supposed to keep away from theological issues. When therefore they were accused of promoting a naturalistic outlook, they could retort that they were simply doing what they were supposed to do, expounding what Aristotle and other philosophers had said. My point is however that, with a few exceptions, most of the creative work in philosophy was done by people who either were theologians or who, like Ockham, aimed at being professors of theology.

This situation meant of course that to a considerable extent the selection and treatment of philosophical problems and themes was influenced by theological considerations and interests. It is indeed possible to exaggerate this influence. As one might expect, some problems arose out of what had been said by other philosophers, whether classical or medieval, or as a result of reflection on permanent features of, say, language, or out of both factors combined. At the same time philosophical themes tended to be treated in a theological setting. Further, with Aquinas and other thirteenth-century theologians philosophical reflection was regarded as culminating at points where a certain overlapping with theology began. Metaphysics, for example, was regarded as culminating in what we would describe as philosophical theology. And even when, as in the Ockhamist movement of the fourteenth century, philosophy and theology tended to fall apart, there was often a mingling of logical and theological considerations, which have to be disentangled.

Consider, for example, Ockham's thesis that from the existence of A we cannot demonstrate the existence of B, when A and B are two distinct things. From one point of view Ockham is speaking as a logician and maintaining that no contradiction is involved if the existence of A is asserted and the existence of B is denied. From another point of view however he is speaking as a theologian and insisting on the divine omnipotence. As God can do anything which does not involve a contradiction, he could in principle maintain A in existence without B's existing, even if in our experience we find that the occurrence of A is regularly followed by the occurrence of B. Here we have logical and theological lines of thought converging to the same conclusion.

The dominating position of theology is of course one of the main features which distinguishes philosophy in the medieval period both from Greek philosophy and from modern philosophy. In the ancient world there was indeed plenty of 'theology' in a broad sense of the word. We have only to think, for instance, of Middle Platonism and Neoplatonism. But there was no dogmatic system of religious beliefs maintained by a teaching Church and serving as a criterion of truth. Though therefore the medievals derived a great deal of their philosophical ideas from the ancient world, a theological superstructure, so to speak, was added to what they inherited from the past, in such a way that the relationship between the two elements was not simply an external one but also influenced the course of philosophical thought in a variety of ways. As for the post-medieval world, it is obvious that as an empirical fact the place of theology as the commonly recognized chief science has been progressively taken over by the particular sciences which have developed since the Middle Ages.

As we are all aware, philosophy has from time to time asserted its own autonomy and independence and tried to find its own special field, as though it was a science distinct from and alongside other sciences. This claim to distinctness and autonomy was indeed recognized to some extent in the Middle Ages. Aquinas, for example, made a reasoned distinction between philosophy, including philosophical theology, on the one hand and what he called 'sacred doctrine' on the other. But for obvious reasons philosophy in the Middle Ages could not play the role of a way of life or even way of salvation which it often played in the ancient world. And in so far as it treated of God and of ethics, it was inevitably subject to the judgment of ecclesiastical authorities and of the theologians. If we wish to find an analogue in the medieval period to attempts to give philosophy a field of its own, it seems to me that the nearest approach that we can find is in the development of logical studies. As has already been noted, in the early Middle Ages philosophy was predominantly, though not entirely, dialectic. In the late Middle Ages logical studies became increasingly prominent, especially when radical criticism was directed against the metaphysical arguments of the theologian-philosophers of the thirteenth century. Philosophy was not identified with logic or with logical analysis. Ockham, for example, did not reject metaphysics. The more however the range of philosophical knowledge was restricted, whether for philosophical or theological reasons or a mixture of both, so much the more did philosophers tend to concentrate on logical studies and on the critical analysis of philosophical ideas and arguments.

2. What I have been saying may seem to imply that the theologian-philosophers of the thirteenth century, men such as
Aquinas, occupied themselves simply with theological and metaphysical themes, paying little attention to logic, while logical
studies flourished only in the fourteenth century, among those
thinkers who were somewhat critical of the metaphysical arguments of their predecessors. This picture of the situation however would be inaccurate. For one thing, philosophical and theological discussion was conducted within a severely logical framework. If we look for example, at the writings of Aquinas, we
find plenty of argumentation but precious little in the way of
purple passages or edifying uplift. And even if, for reasons
which are perhaps none too clear, the poet Gerard Manley
Hopkins was much attracted by Duns Scotus, it would be waste
of time to look for imaginative and poetical flights in the works
of the medieval thinker whose name has become associated with
the drawing of fine and subtle distinctions. For another thing,
it was the theologians of the thirteenth century who first made
use of what was then called the 'new' logic, the logical ideas
made available through the translation into Latin of those
books of Aristotle's *Organon* which were not comprised in the
books, such as the *Categories* and *De Interpretatione*, that made
up the so-called 'old' logic. As for the 'modern' logic, which was
contrasted with the 'ancient' logic (comprising both the 'old'
and the 'new' logics in the sense mentioned above), this was
characterized by the attention paid to analyzing the functions
of terms in propositions. It began in the thirteenth century but
was developed of course in the fourteenth, being associated particularly with the theory of 'supposition' (the theory of the substantive term's function of standing for things in the proposition), as found, for instance, in the logical writings of William of
Ockham. As for fourteenth-century criticism of previous metaphysical arguments, this often took the form of pressing the
concept of demonstration as found in Aristotle's *Posterior
Analytics* and maintaining that this or that argument did not
exemplify the concept which was accepted by the Greek philosopher.

What is customarily described as symbolic or mathematical
logic is of course a development of modern times. The medieval

logicians can perhaps be said to have developed a semi-artificial language, in the sense that they used a number of technical terms. But they wrote in the ordinary language of academic discourse, namely Latin. It would however be rash to conclude that the medievals did not understand that logic is a formal science and that they muddled up logic and ontology. To be sure, we can find instances of this. Thus in the ninth century a certain Fredegisius of Tours seems to have supposed that there must be some reality corresponding to the word 'nothing', and to have drawn the conclusion that God must have created the world out of a pre-existing undifferentiated material, on the lines, we may assume, of the divine craftsman's behaviour in Plato's *Timaeus*. But in the eleventh century St Anselm pointed out that the statement that God created the world out of nothing is equivalent to saying that he did not create it out of anything. In other words, he anticipated, in regard to a particular instance at any rate, Bertrand Russell's distinction between the grammatical and logical forms of a proposition. As for the formal character of logic, in the early part of the twelfth century Abelard was clearly turning away from the idea of logic as treating of entities, including mental entities, to the idea of it as concerned with terms, propositions and forms of inference. Obviously, the idea of logic as a propaedeutic to the various sciences or disciplines favoured the conception of logic as being in itself a formal study. And if we look at the logical treatises of the second half of the thirteenth century and of the fourteenth century, we can see, for example, that when they treated of inferential operations they were considering formal relations, and that the formal validity of an argument did not entail the truth of the conclusion. The terminist logic was a logic of terms, of the functions of terms in propositions and of the relations between propositions, not of things. The logicians may give the impression of being largely concerned with grammar. But a distinction was made between logic on the one hand and 'speculative grammar' on the other. What the medievals called speculative grammar aimed at laying bare an essential structure which was conceived as underlying the grammatical forms of different particular languages and as reflecting a basic ontological structure. Whatever one may think about this enterprise, speculative grammar was distinct from formal logic and seems to have faded away in the second half of the fourteenth century.

It is perhaps worth mentioning Ockham's classification of logic as a rational, as distinct from a real science. If it were stated in modern English that logic is not a real science, the statement would most probably be understood as meaning that logic is not a science at all. But if anyone proposes to study medieval philosophy, he has to learn the language, the terminology that is to say. In Ockham's view anything, by the very fact that it exists, is individual. It does not require anything to individuate it. There are not, and cannot be, universal entities or things. Science however is concerned with propositions. And in these propositions certain terms 'stand for' individuals. In a statement about the human body, for example, the general term 'human body' stands for individual human bodies. Universality is a function of terms in propositions. Anatomy is thus a 'real' science, inasmuch as 'body' stands for bodies. If however I say that species are subdivisions of genuses, the term 'species' stands for 'man', 'lion', 'horse' and so on, terms which in themselves stand for things. In other words logic treats of terms or concepts which stand for other terms or concepts, not directly for things. And in this sense it is a 'rational' and not a 'real' science. Ockham draws of course further distinctions. For example, he has to allow for the distinction between logic and grammar. To use the term 'lion' as standing for lions is not the same thing as to use it as standing for itself, as in the sentence '*lion* is a noun'. But I cannot pursue the matter here.

What I have been saying may seem to imply that for Ockham logic does treat of things, but indirectly. And I suppose that there is a sense in which this is true. But in elaborating the theory of 'supposition' or 'standing for' Ockham is concerned with showing that universality is a function of terms in propositions, not of things. And the 'formal object' or particular subject-matter of logic is for him terms and propositions and the relations between them. When he speaks, for instance, of 'formal consequences', he is referring to implication which is governed by a logical rule that is concerned solely with the logical form or structure of the relevant propositions, and not with their content.

From the thirteenth century logicians took a notable interest in paradoxes and logical puzzles. One such puzzle was provided by the statement 'what I am saying is false'. If we assume that nothing else whatsoever is said, the proposition seems to be self-referring. That is to say, the statement 'what I am saying is false' implies of itself that it is false. And in this case it must be true. Ockham's way of dealing with this puzzle was to claim that the proposition could not be self-referring. Buridan however would not accept this solution; and he suggested, at one time at any rate, that any proposition, in virtue of its nature, implies its own truth. If therefore a proposition is such that it both asserts and denies its own truth, it must be false.

The attention paid by the logicians of the Middle Ages to logical puzzles is doubtless partly responsible for the impression that they were preoccupied with 'trivialities', an impression summed up in the statement which has sometimes been made that medieval philosophers spent their time debating how many angels could dance at the same time on the point of a pin. This picture of their activities is in any case a caricature. As for the particular question referred to, I am not aware that its discussion has actually been verified. The question may indeed have been discussed, as a matter of light entertainment, at one of those more informal disputations at which any problems (*quaestiones quodlibetales*) could be raised. Given however the medievals' belief about angels as spiritual beings, the only proper answer would be that the question was a pseudo-question.

3. As discussion of logical themes was a prominent feature of medieval philosophy, I do not think that any apology is required for referring to the topic. It is time however that I turned to some other aspects of medieval thought, even if my remarks are inevitably brief and inadequate.

The first point which I would like to make is that the position given to St Thomas Aquinas in the Roman Catholic Church from the publication of Pope Leo XIII's *Aeterni Patris* in 1879 until recently, together with the development of the Neo-Thomist movement, as represented, for example, by Jacques Maritain, has contributed to the creation of a one-sided picture of medieval philosophy. Aquinas was indeed an eminent theologian and philosopher, but at no time in the Middle Ages did he occupy the position which he has enjoyed in modern times. Medieval philosophy is not synonymous with the thought of Aquinas. It is far more varied. To be sure, if we looked to the Middle Ages for a succession of different world-views, such as those of Spinoza, Berkeley, Schelling, Hegel,

Schopenhauer, Nietzsche, Whitehead and Sartre, we would be disappointed. Within however the limits set by a background of common religious beliefs, there was room for a measure of variety which tends to be overlooked if the philosophy of the Middle Ages is interpreted as consisting of a preparation for the thought of Aquinas and then, after Aquinas, as a decline.

Let me apply what I have just said to the topic of arguments for the existence of God. It is probably true to say that for many people medieval thought on this subject was pretty well confined to St Anselm's famous argument in the *Proslogion* and to Aquinas's Five Ways, which were summaries or developments of other people's lines of thought. If however we look at the somewhat forbidding writings of the Scottish thinker Duns Scotus, we find a somewhat different attitude from that of Aquinas. Aquinas starts with experienced facts. Thus in the First Way he asserts as certain that some things in the world are moved (undergo change that is to say), while in the Third Way he takes it that we know by experience that some things at any rate are capable of being or not being, inasmuch as they are evidently subject to generation and corruption. Scotus does not suggest that such statements are false. For they are pretty obviously true. What Scotus maintains is that all factual propositions relating to finite things are contingent. If true, they are contingently true. If therefore these contingently true propositions are used as a basis for proving the existence of God, the conclusion will itself be contingently true. He prefers to argue from the *possibility* of the existence of things. In other words, he tries to show, by means of a complex and lengthy argument, that the existence of God is the ultimate and necessary condition of the possibility of there being any finite thing at all. He assumes of course that while the existence of finite things is not necessary, the possibility of their existing is. We can recall to mind that in his 'pre-critical' work, *The Only Possible Ground for a Demonstration of God's Existence*, Immanuel Kant argued in much the same way. We cannot deny possibility without thinking; and to think is to affirm implicitly the realm of possibility. Possibility however requires an ultimate existent ground.

It may be objected that even if this line of argument is valid, an ultimate ground of possibility is not at all what Christians mean by God. Scotus would doubtless reply that though the Christian concept of God comprises much more than the idea of a ground of possibility, it none the less includes it. Besides, while Aquinas had maintained that the doctrine of the Trinity was a truth of faith and not a matter of philosophy, Scotus further restricted the range of what could be philosophically proved by relegating several divine attributes to the sphere of faith. In other words, in the philosophy of the late Middle Ages there was a tendency to narrow the limits of what the philosopher could prove about the nature of God. Indeed, when we find Ockham relegating the divine unicity to the sphere of faith, it becomes doubtful to what extent we can still speak of proving the existence of God. Ockham does indeed maintain that there must be a supreme conserving cause of this world. But as he admits that, for all the philosopher knows, there might be other worlds, with other supreme conserving causes, I find some difficulty in sharing the confidence of Dr Boehner that Ockham looked on the existence of God as philosophically demonstrable.

It is possible of course to look on the ideas to which I have alluded from various points of view. For example, it could be argued that whereas Aquinas, in his proofs of the existence of God, made unexamined and uncriticized assumptions, Duns Scotus tried to develop a more rigorous proof. As for the tendency in late medieval thought to restrict the range of metaphysical knowledge and to take refuge in 'fideism', the Thomists have generally regarded it as a manifestation of a regrettable decline into nominalism or what not. But it is also possible to regard it as the manifestation of a better idea of what is required to constitute a proof. In any case my main aim is to illustrate the fact that in spite of the background of commonly shared religious beliefs there was a considerable measure of variety in medieval philosophy.

4. Criticism of other people's arguments is a favourite pastime of philosophers. And in this respect the medieval philosophers were certainly not uncritical. Nor was it simply a case of maintaining that there were formal defects in this or that argument according to the standards of Aristotelian logic. When, for example, Aquinas attacked the theory of the unicity of the human intellect by arguing that the theory could not account for the obvious fact that two human beings can very well think differently and have different ideas and convictions, he was making a

substantial point. He may have neglected the fact (doubtless through being unaware of it) that Averroes, the eminent Moslem philosopher, had anticipated this objection and tried to meet it. But Aquinas was not complaining that the mono-psychists' syllogisms were faulty. He was arguing that their theory was at variance with empirical facts. Similarly, when Duns Scotus citicized the argument for human immortality based on a natural desire to continue in life, he was not simply attacking the argument from the point of view of a formal logician. He pointed out that if it was a matter of a biological tendency or instinct to avoid what was felt to be threatening or destructive, this instinct could be found in animals as well as in human beings and could not therefore be cited in support of the thesis that human beings, but not animals, enjoy immortality. If however it was a matter of a conscious desire to survive death, it should be remembered that human beings can perfectly well desire ends which they cannot attain. If we wish to argue that the desire will be fulfilled, we must first show that it *can* be fulfilled.

The attitude shown by Scotus in discussing arguments for immortality is certainly not uncritical. And in the first half of the fourteenth century some thinkers, such as Nicholas of Autrecourt, pursued critical lines of thought of such a radical character that, if accepted as valid, it would undermine a great deal of medieval metaphysics. It is not without reason that Nicholas of Autrecourt has been described as the medieval Hume. At the same time it might be argued that though the medieval philosophers were by no means uncritical of one another's arguments, they were none the less uncritical in the sense that they all made assumptions which remained unexamined precisely because they were common assumptions. For example, though they treated of knowledge from a psychological point of view, they did not really raise the question whether we can know anything at all or whether, if we can know, our knowledge is confined to our own ideas and impressions. Realism was a common assumption; and it was an uncritical or naive realism.

It is obviously true that the medieval philosophers were pre-critical in the sense that they lived long before Immanuel Kant. It is also true, I imagine, that they would have had a good deal of sympathy with the robust common-sense realism of G.E. Moore. But it would be inaccurate to say that they all assumed a realist position in a naive manner. For example, Aquinas main-

tained that we know that we can know by first knowing something, or that we can understand by first understanding something and then understanding that we understood. Some philosophers might describe this position as uncritical, but it seems
to me to be a quite respectable position. Indeed, how else could
we establish our capacity to know except by reflecting on our
knowledge? There is of course the possibility of error, of
making false judgments which we do not know to be false. But
the ways of correcting error are the ways which we actually use.
When Aquinas says, in his *De Veritate*, that we have to have recourse to first principles, this may sound as though he meant
that to solve our perplexities we must have recourse to self-
evidently true premises and pursue a path of logical deduction.
But under 'first principles' he includes actual sense-perception.
If I am in doubt whether what I see in the gloaming is a human
body or the stump of a tree, taking the matter back to 'first
principles' means, in this context, having a closer look. This
may be a naive attitude, but it is doubtful whether a philosopher could find any more effective way of settling the doubt.

As for subjective idealism, in the sense of the doctrine that
what we know directly are our own ideas or impressions, it is
true that in their psychological account of knowledge the medieval philosophers talked a lot about images and concepts. They
were however conscious of the possible interpretation that the
direct objects of our knowledge are mental entities. And some
of them tried in their various ways to avoid this implication.
Thus Aquinas was careful to maintain that the concept was a
medium quo, a means by which we know a thing, not a *medium
quod*, the object of knowledge. And after Aquinas there was a
distinct tendency, as with Ockham, to get rid of psychical or
mental entities whenever possible. For Ockham the universal
concept was not a mental entity standing, as it were, between
subject and object but simply a way of conceiving individual
things abstractly, while for Durandus knowing was simply a
direct relation between the mind and its object, whatever the
object might be. If it is a case of knowing a human person, it is
the person whom I know, not some modification of my mind.
The various positions adopted by the medieval philosophers on
such matters may not have been developed to the extent
to which a modern philosopher would try to develop them.
But they were at any rate aware of the fact that their talk about

images and concepts gave rise to the question whether these mental entities constituted the direct objects of our knowledge.

The medieval philosophers, I have argued, were quite capable of recognizing problems which arose out of the language which they employed. For example, if science is said to be concerned with universal concepts, does it follow that science treats of mental entities or of 'accidental' modifications of the mind? If not, are we to say that science treats of things inasmuch as universal concepts represent essences existing in things? Or are we to say with Ockham that the 'real' sciences treat of things inasmuch as universal concepts 'stand for' things in universal statements? Again, if we predicate of God terms which we apply in the first instance to creatures and the meaning of which is determined by our experience of, say, human beings, in what sense can such terms be predicated of an infinite invisible transcendent reality? If the terms are applied in the same sense in which they are applied to human beings for instance, it seems to follow that God must be conceived as a kind of invisible superman. If however the terms are applied in a totally different sense, they seem to be evacuated of all assignable meaning. What therefore is one to say? Aquinas and Scotus, for example, tried to solve this sort of problem, though in rather different ways.

Again, it would be inaccurate to claim that the medieval thinkers were incapable of challenging presuppositions. If someone accepts either Hume's account or Kant's account of the causal relation, he is likely to maintain that Aquinas assumed uncritically that the idea of causation could be used to transcend phenomena, as in his causal proof of God's existence. However this may be, the fact remains that in the fourteenth century Nicholas of Autrecourt, and some other philosophers, maintained that we can never demonstrate the existence of one thing from the existence of another, though experience of regular sequence warrants our expecting that B will follow A in the future. This line of thought would seem to rule out any causal proof of God's existence. For the question of experiencing a regular sequence hardly arises in this case.

Though however it would be inaccurate to suggest that the medieval philosophers were incapable of detecting and challenging presuppositions, it by no means follows that there were not common beliefs which were not subjected to criticism. The most obvious case is doubtless to be found in the field of religious belief. Aquinas rejected St Anselm's proof of the existence of God as given in the *Proslogion*. Duns Scotus, as we have seen, preferred an approach which was rather different from that of Aquinas. The more radical thinkers of the fourteenth century greatly restricted the limits of what the human reason could prove about God; and, even if they did not say so explicitly, they adopted positions from which it would follow that the existence of God could not be proved in any strict sense. In other words, more and more was relegated to the sphere of faith. It would be a complete mistake to think, for instance, that Ockham was not a believer. It was a case of the growth of 'fideism' rather than of unbelief. And the adoption of a fideist attitude was often inspired, in part that is to say, by a religious motive, the desire to free Christian belief from what was regarded as the disfiguring contamination of Greco-Islamic metaphysics. The fact remains however that the thinkers who relegated truths relating to God to the spheres of relevation and the response of faith did not pursue any serious reflection on the grounds for believing that what was claimed to be revelation actually was what it was claimed to be. It is not a question of blaming them for this. In any culture there are likely to be beliefs, not necessarily religious beliefs of course, which are assumed as a background for intellectual activity. Besides, it is not as though the beliefs in question were the result of proofs of the existence of God as presented by Anselm, Aquinas, Scotus or anyone else. The religious beliefs antedated these proofs. The arguments were advanced within, so to speak, the area of faith. And when the arguments were subjected to criticism, the faith remained. Though however the situation is perfectly understandable, it seems to me clearly true that in this field the medieval philosophers can reasonably be regarded as uncritical. It can indeed be added that while some fourteenth-century philosophers, such as Ockham, were quite clearly convinced believers, there are some others who might perhaps have subjected the background of faith to questioning and criticism, had they felt it prudent to do so. But we have no means of deciding this issue. That is to say, there are cases in which we lack the necessary evidence for assessing the sincerity of protestations of faith made by philosophers who otherwise manifested a radically critical attitude. If we assume that these thinkers were sincere, we can only conclude that there was a point at which their critical questioning was brought to a halt.

A good many modern theologians would claim that faith stands in no need of philosophical justification. It is a human being's response to the divine self-disclosure. God reveals himself, not propositions. The relevant propositions are the fruit of the community's reflection on and interpretation of religious experience, encounter with God. In terms of philosophy the language of faith is an autonomous language-game which expresses and forms part of a way of life which needs no justification from outside. Indeed, there can be no such justification. Nor can there be any justifiable criticism of first-order religious language. For there are no neutral criteria in terms of which the language of faith could be either criticized or justified. It is *sui generis*. Conversion, not argumentation, constitutes the point of entry to the relevant form of life.

It is not my intention to discuss this point of view on its own merits or demerits. I am concerned with the medieval thinkers. And I wish simply to draw attention to the following points. First, if we look at the writings of Aquinas, we find him saying that whereas philosophy bases itself on premises known by the natural light of reason, 'sacred doctrine' is based on revealed premises. That certain premises are revealed is simply accepted as part of the common background of belief. Secondly, though Aquinas believed that a doctrine such as the Trinity was beyond the reach of philosophical faith, he was at pains to argue that such doctrines were not self-contradictory. This point of view would not, I think, be compatible with the theory of autonomous language-games in its extreme form. For it is implied that the principle of non-contradiction transcends the boundaries between language-games. Thirdly, in the fourteenth century we do indeed find an English Dominican, Robert Holcot, asserting that ordinary logic does not apply in the sphere of faith and that there is need for a 'logic of faith' which, apparently, transcends the principles of identity and non-contradiction. If we like, we can see here an embryonic anticipation of the theory of ʲautonomousˡlanguage-games. But, as far as I am aware, the nature of this 'logic of faith' was not worked out.

All that I am saying is that in medieval thought there was an area which was left unexamined, even by those philosophers who otherwise pursued a policy of pretty radical questioning. I dare say that ecclesiastical authoritarianism had something to do with this. But it is not a sufficient explanation. For, if taken as a sufficient explanation, it implies that an absence of radical questioning in regard to the rationality of religious faith was due simply to timorous prudence. And this was clearly not the case. A late medieval thinker such as Ockham was undoubtedly a sincere believer. But he seems to have lacked any clear view of the problems arising out of his own restriction of the range of philosophical knowledge. One main reason for this was doubtless the general background of faith, which constituted a commonly accepted premise or presupposition. The situation is obviously different today. But there may be other presuppositions. A good many people seem to work on the implicit assumption that to exist means to be a possible object of sense-experience. In other words, to grasp and examine one's own presuppositions, those which one makes in common with others, is not so easy. Perhaps, as Ortega y Gasset maintained, every culture has its presuppositions or beliefs which are only later subjected to critical questioning.

5. Within the framework of commonly held beliefs, the medieval philosophers dealt seriously with a variety of problems. The ways in which the problems arose were of course historically conditioned. And it is doubtless true that some of the problems treated seem entirely alien to us, inasmuch as they arose in the context of hypotheses which are no longer current. For example, as we do not think in terms of a hierarchy of celestial spheres, each of which is moved by an intelligence, we cannot be expected to take a passionate interest in questions about the number of intelligences or about the function which some medievals thought to be performed in the human mind by the lowest intelligence in the hierarchy. It would however be a mistake to conceive the medieval thinker's view of the world simply in terms of a hierarchy of spheres and angelic movers. For in the fourteenth century the theory of impetus was developed, by Buridan and Albert of Saxony for example, according to which the Creator imposed on the heavenly bodies at creation a certain impetus or energy. The proponents of this theory spoke with some caution, it is true. But the theory clearly implied that there was no need at all for the hypothesis of movers of the spheres. For if the heavenly bodies encountered no resistance, they would continue to move in virtue of the

originally imparted impetus. In other words, the theory paved the way for a mechanical view of the world as a system of bodies in motion, motion or energy being transmitted from one body to another. To be sure, talk about the conferring and transmission of impetus seems to imply that impetus is an entity. And there was some discussion about how it should be classified in terms of the Aristotelian theory of categories. In point of fact Ockham, with his characteristic determination to eliminate superfluous entities, had maintained that a moving body moves simply because it is in motion. My point is however that within the medieval period itself the ground was prepared for the Cartesian view of the material world as a mechanical system. The medieval thinkers suffered of course from scientific ignorance, but they were not such prisoners as is sometimes supposed of a certain cosmology. For the matter of that, Nicholas of Oresme in the fourteenth century produced some excellent reasons in favour of the hypothesis that it is the earth which rotates daily rather than that the sun goes round a stationary earth. In his discussion of the matter he makes it clear that he regards scientific theories as hypotheses, and that in his opinion the theory of the earth's rotation is the more economical hypothesis. He also makes the point that the Bible uses the ordinary way of speaking and should not be used to settle scientific issues. In the end however he opts for the traditional hypothesis, possibly out of prudence.

There is another point which is perhaps worth making. We are apt to think of medieval philosophy as consisting predominantly of metaphysical themes, pursued in subordination to theological ends. And it is true of course both that metaphysical discussion was a prominent feature of medieval thought and that it was carried on mainly by theologians, such as Anselm, Bonaventure, Aquinas and Duns Scotus. But we can also find the emergence of a tendency to convert ontological or metaphysical distinctions into distinctions relating to language. An example of this sort of thing is provided by Ockham's handling of the alleged real distinction between essence and existence. It may be the case, as Dr D. H. Henry has suggested, that Ockham is unfair to certain other medieval philosophers by interpreting in terms of ordinary language a distinction which they understood in a more technical sense. That is to say, in ordinary language talk about a real distinction would probably be understood as referring to a distinction between distinct things, whereas when Aquinas said or implied that there was a real distinction between essence and existence, he meant that essence and existence were two really distinguishable metaphysical components in one thing, not that they were distinct things. But I imagine that Ockham was thinking primarily of writers such as Giles of Rome and Henry of Ghent, rather than of Aquinas. Not that this matters for my present purpose. I am concerned with drawing attention to the fact that Ockham's way of handling the issue is to maintain that essence and existence signify the same thing, the one in the manner of a noun, the other (esse) in the manner of a verb. As their linguistic functions are different, the terms cannot be used interchangeably; but it by no means follows that they signify distinct realities.

Another example is Ockham's treatment of the belief that there is a sphere of possible entities, distinct from the world of actual entities. He interprets the distinction between possibility and act as a matter of the modality of assertions. To say that Tom has a son is different from saying that he could have one. But it does not follow that there is a possible son which is half-way, so to speak, between not-being and actual existence.

Ockham's treatment of such matters is not inspired by any hostility towards metaphysics as such. Nor even by a peculiar mania for reducing the population of the universe. He is convinced that our use of abstract terms gives rise to the temptation to think that there must be corresponding entities, and that language, to use a Wittgensteinian expression, can exercise a bewitching and misleading influence. We speak, for example, of events happening 'in time'. And we may therefore be inclined to postulate a reality called 'time' which constitutes the medium in which events occur. Hence the need for an analysis of the concept of time or of temporal expressions which can show us that to postulate a reality called 'time' which is distinct from things and the human mind is to make an unnecessary or superfluous postulate. Reductive analysis of this kind is for Ockham itself a metaphysical activity, inasmuch as it displays reality as consisting simply of individual things and their absolute accidents.

6. By selecting such a broad theme as 'Some Aspects of Medieval Philosophy' I committed myself in advance to what has

been, I fear, a rather impressionistic treatment, in which no one particular topic could be developed in depth. My excuse for this procedure is that though nowadays medieval philosophy is less neglected than it used to be, it is not widely studied in our universities, not, that is to say, in comparison with Greek philosophy up to and including Aristotle and with the development of philosophy from Descartes onwards. One reason for this is probably a conviction that medieval philosophy was pursued in subordination to theology and to theological ends, and that the philosophers of the Middle Ages, however talented some of them may have been, were preoccupied with questions which are no longer actual. Though however this conception of medieval philosophy is not devoid of foundation of fact, I have tried to show that there was considerable variety in medieval thought, and that some of the lines of thought which we tend to regard as characteristic of recent philosophy had their analogues in the Middle Ages.

By saying this I do not intend to imply that history repeats itself in a literal sense. Nor do I wish to be understood as implying that present-day British philosophy provides an absolute standard of judgment which entitles us to award good marks to medieval philosophers simply in so far as they approximated to later ideas of what philosophers should be doing. I no more think this than I advocate a return to the Middle Ages. In other words, my interest is mainly historical.

Here too a qualification is required. I am indeed convinced that as philosophy does not simply pursue an isolated path of its own but is one among other cultural activities, it is historically conditioned in a variety of ways. It does not follow however that the historical conditioning is such that nothing of permanent value is said. Consider, for example, political or social philosophy, of which I have said nothing in the course of this chapter. It is obvious that in so far as a medieval thinker was concerned with the particular society in which he lived, his thought was historically conditioned, just as the political theories of Plato and Aristotle were historically conditioned. At the same time, when the medieval thinkers insisted, for instance, that government should aim at the common good, they were doubtless enunciating a principle which can be accepted in all periods. The trouble is of course that its timeless validity, so to speak, is accompanied by a notable vagueness. The more abstract the sphere, the more likely are we to find positions which are not tied to a given historical situation. And it is arguable, I suppose, that conceptual analysis provides the most promising field for finding positions which are not indissolubly linked to the structure of medieval culture.

Political theory has just been mentioned as an area which has been left untouched in this chapter. Another such area is ethics. In this area it is interesting to speculate what the medieval philosophers would have said, had they been taxed with committing the naturalistic fallacy. This question arises in connection with Aquinas's concept of the natural moral law and, in a somewhat different way, in the context of Ockham's ethical authoritarianism, his relating, that is to say, of the moral law to the divine will. But I cannot pursue this particular hare at the close of this chapter.

CHAPTER V

REFLECTIONS ON ANALYTIC PHILOSOPHY

It seems safe to say that both analysis and synthesis are permanent features of theoretical activity, of the process of understanding, and that, as such, they do not stand in need of any special justification. We can regard both procedures as involving presuppositions. Analysis presupposes that there are complex phenomena, whereas synthesis presupposes that things are related in various ways. These presuppositions are however grounded in experience and confirmed by it, and on the level of common sense we are convinced of the truth of both.

Philosophers can indeed emphasize one activity rather than the other. For example, in his *Principles of Logic* F.H. Bradley maintained that analysis distorts reality, whereas Bertrand Russell was prepared to assert that reductive analysis is the path to knowledge of reality. What however these two philosophers said about analysis and synthesis was determined to a large extent by their respective philosophical positions.[1] In point of fact both men employed analysis and synthesis.[2] As philosophers they could hardly do otherwise.

In the so-called analytic movement emphasis has been placed, as the adjective indicates, on analysis. There has been a strong tendency to mistrust large-scale or comprehensive syntheses and to insist on the need for making questions or problems as precise as possible, on breaking up portmanteau problems into their distinguishable components, and on treating each of them separately. In the course of time however the interlocking of problems has been more clearly recognized, and a movement towards synthesis has reasserted itself. Thus in so far as the descriptive term 'the analytic movement' is justified, it seems to me to be now a matter of emphasis rather than of any dogmatic exclusion of synthesis as such.

It is not my intention to treat in this paper of the analytic movement as a whole. I am concerned with the approach to philosophy by way of reflection on ordinary language.[3] And I propose to treat briefly both of the presuppositions of ordinary language philosophy and of the question whether this sort of philosophizing is concerned only with words. In the *Theses on*

100

Feuerbach Marx made his famous statement that philosophers had hitherto only interpreted the world, whereas the point was to change it. Obviously, Marx was not blaming the philosophers for trying to interpret the word. His contention was that interpretation, theory, was insufficient. Some critics however have suggested that the so-called linguistic analysts do not even interpret the world but are concerned exclusively with words. I wish to examine this suggestion.

2. What is meant by the term 'ordinary language'? To mention one or two things which it does not mean is easy enough. The term does not refer to the speech of the less well educated as contrasted with that of more highly educated persons. Nor does it refer exclusively to the English language, as distinct from, say, Greek or German or French.[4] If however the concept of ordinary language is to have any definite content or meaning it must be contrasted with something. With what is it contrasted?

In the first place, it seems to me, it excludes any model or allegedly perfect language consciously and deliberately created by logicians, a language in which the uses or meanings of all symbols would be clearly defined and which would be free from the ambiguities and other 'deficiencies' of language as it actually exists. In the second place the term seems sometimes to be used in such a way as to exclude the technical language not so much of non-philosophical disciplines, such as physics, psychology and theology, as of philosophy itself. Thus in an article entitled 'Ordinary Language' Gilbert Ryle uses the term in both senses.[5]

The second interpretation may imply that philosophy has no special field of its own, and that philosophers have therefore no special substantive knowledge, increase in which drives them to develop a technical vocabulary in a manner analogous to that in which the physicist invents technical terms to express new hypotheses in, say, nuclear physics. What the philosopher does is to use ordinary words, such as 'knowledge', in special senses which he claims to be their real meaning or what they ought to mean. The ordinary language analyst wants to get away from such philosophical theories and to look at the ways in which words actually function.

The assumption that philosophy has no special field of its own is clearly one which might be challenged by some of those philosophers who would none the less agree that not all philosophical disputes can be settled by translating them into a deliberately constructed notation or model language, and who would thus be prepared to contrast ordinary language with a purely 'artificial' (consciously and deliberately constructed) language. But we can leave aside this assumption for the moment. I have simply been trying to give some indication of what analytic philosophers understand by the term 'ordinary language'.

3. The concentration on language which has been a characteristic feature of what is sometimes described as 'Oxford philosophy' naturally tends to give the impression that the relevant philosophers are concerned 'only with words'. No great amount of reflection is required however to see that this impression is incorrect. Consider, for example, the well-known work *The Concept of Mind*,[6] written by Gilbert Ryle, one of the foremost practitioners of ordinary language philosophy. In his book Ryle is constantly drawing our attention to what people are accustomed to say. As I have remarked elsewhere however, "it would be absurd to say that the book is about words. It is about *man*".[7] Professor A.J. Ayer puts the matter well when he says that 'when we examine what we should say when, what words we the ghost in the machine, he tries to make us fix our attention on the actual phenomena of what is supposed to be our mental life'.[8] Again, J.L. Austin, who, if anyone, was concerned with mapping out the forms of ordinary language, asserted that 'when we examine what we should say when, what words we should use in what situations, we are looking again not *merely* at words . . . but also at the realities we use the words to talk about'.[9]

Consider David Hume on causality. He is obviously not talking about the English word 'cause' in the manner of a philologist. Nor is he talking about the word 'cause' in a way which would exclude its German or French equivalent. He is inquiring into the concept of cause. And this inquiry includes reflection on the objective reference of the concept, of what William of Ockham called the *terminus conceptus*. Similarly, Gilbert Ryle is not concerned simply with the words 'mind' and 'body'. He is concerned with the concepts. True, in order to elucidate the concepts he appeals to the concrete utterances of ordinary language. But his aim is surely to make us see more clearly what man is. Whether we agree or not with Ryle's account of man is irrelevant to this particular point.

It might however be objected that even if the ordinary language philosophers are not concerned simply with words, they none the less focus attention on what people are accustomed to say about things or phenomena. Why not go directly to things, to the facts, and let them speak for themselves? What is the point of paying so much attention to ordinary language which, according to Bertrand Russell, embodies the metaphysics of the Stone Age? Is it perhaps assumed that ordinary language is an infallible criterion of truth?

In regard to the utility or point of an examination of and reflection on ordinary language, a good deal depends on the way in which we understand the term 'ordinary language'. If we contrast ordinary language simply with an allegedly perfect or model symbolic language deliberately constructed by logicians, the language of science, for instance, falls within the field of ordinary language. And in this case the point of reflecting on ordinary language seems to be clear enough. For what can the philosopher of science do but reflect on what scientists say or, if preferred, on the concepts expressed in what they say and on the presuppositions, if any, of what they say? The philosopher of science does not attempt to rival the scientist in his own field. He must start from what scientists actually say. If however we understand ordinary language in a sense which would exclude from its area the technical vocabulary or concepts of physicists, psychologists, theologians and so on, the situation is rather different. An appeal to ordinary language would clearly be irrelevant to settling issues in, for instance, nuclear physics. But it would by no means follow that an appeal to ordinary language was useless in all areas. Consider, for instance, the problem of freedom, in a psychological sense that is to say, freedom of the will, to use a common expression. Everyday language provides a rich variety of types of utterance which express different degrees of voluntariness and involuntariness. 'I could not help dropping the cup; I was struck violently on the arm'. 'I did not intend to drop the cup; but I did not notice the hole in the carpet, and I tripped'. 'Yes, I admit that I dropped the cup; but I had just been grossly insulted, and I lost my temper'. 'Yes, I dropped the cup, and I did so deliberately. I wanted to divert attention from what X was saying. I thought of several things which I could do. I decided to throw down the cup and smash it, making as much noise as possible'. Let us suppose that a philosopher points out how here we have various types of assertion, ranging from a statement about the use of physical force, through statements referring to excuses or diminished responsibility, to a frank confession of deliberate intention. And let us suppose that the philosopher goes on to argue that such distinctions in ordinary language have developed in response to man's experience of himself and of his behaviour through the centuries. The philosopher argues that such distinctions are there, in our language, because we need them. They are not arbitrary constructions but correspond with familiar objective situations. This sort of argument is surely not pointless. It draws attention to phenomena which need to be taken into consideration in any discussion of human freedom. We need to be able to distinguish between physical compulsion, diminished responsibility and fully deliberate action. And we need to be able to do so, because there are different objective situations which not only warrant but demand it.

It will immediately be objected of course that we cannot prove that man is free by appealing to ordinary language. There are obviously differences between actions which are the result of physical compulsion, actions which are performed under the influence of passion or strong emotion, and actions which are performed deliberately in view of a clearly conceived goal or end. Ordinary language gives expression to these distinctions in concrete ways. But it does not follow that because a man performed action *a* with the deliberate intention of attaining goal *y*, he could have acted otherwise than he did. If this is what freedom is taken to mean, no appeal to ordinary language can prove that man is free. For the feeling of freedom may be, as Spinoza maintained, the result of ignorance of the determining causes. In fine, ordinary language is not an infallible criterion of truth.

No, it is not. But it is a mistake to think that the philosophers of ordinary language claim that it is. Let me quote a brief passage by J. L. Austin. 'Ordinary language is *not* the last word; in principle it can everywhere be supplemented and improved upon and superseded. Only remember, it is the *first* word'.[10] What Austin means by claiming that ordinary language has the first word can be seen easily enough by considering the problem which I have mentioned above, the problem of freedom. Instead of jumping at once to some theory of his own the philosopher would do well to examine and reflect on man's experience of himself throughout a long period of time, an experience which finds concrete expression in ordinary language. It is reasonable to argue that the philosopher should start here, by examining as wide a range as possible of relevant utterances and by reflecting on their implications. He may indeed come to the conclusion, on subsequent reflection, that the views of human action which are implicit in ordinary language are inadequate or stand in need of correction or revision. But he ought at least to examine them first. Otherwise he runs the risk of propounding some theory which rides roughshod over distinctions which human experience has found it necessary to express. Austin certainly thought that ordinary language embodied something better than the metaphysics of the Stone Age, but he did not claim that it had the last word or that it was an infallible criterion of truth.

5. An admission that ordinary language may stand in need of revision or correction does not necessarily entail the claim that philosophy can supply the needed revision or correction. A philosopher may indeed claim to be able to do this. But he is not logically compelled to do so simply because he admits that ordinary language is not an ultimate criterion of truth. This can be seen by considering once more the theme of human freedom. It would be possible for a philosopher to maintain that the implicit assumptions of ordinary language in this area are in principle open to revision or correction, and then add that any grounds for such revision or correction must be brought by the physiologist or psychologist, by empirical science that is to say, and not by philosophy. For while the scientist can discover hitherto unknown facts, the philosopher is not in a position to do this.

The question arises therefore whether ordinary language philosophy involves the assumption that the philosopher can do no more than draw attention to what in a sense we already knew, to what is already before us in ordinary language, and that any correction of ordinary language must be the result of scientific discovery or hypothesis.[11] If this is in fact an assumption, is not ordinary language philosophy a kind of linguistic positivism?[12]

Whether the assumption in question is or is not made by the ordinary language philosopher obviously depends to some extent on how we understand the phrase 'ordinary language philosopher'. If we describe in this way anyone who approaches philosophical questions by way of reflection on ordinary language, using it as a point of departure when it seems to be relevant, it hardly needs saying that the assumption is not necessarily involved. In his *Ethics* Aristotle appealed to what was commonly said on the ground that what everybody or nearly everybody says, in this area at any rate, cannot be altogether wrong. But Aristotle certainly did not think that the philosopher's job was or should be confined to the mapping out of ordinary language. In other words, the ordinary language approach to philosophy does not necessarily involve any other assumption than that it is wise to start by looking at what people are accustomed to say, when this can reasonably be regarded as an embodiment of man's experience of objective situations over a very long period of time. If however we understand the phrase 'ordinary language philosopher' as meaning one who holds, with Ludwig Wittgenstein, that it is not the philosopher's job to change or reform language, but that he 'can in the end only describe it'.[13] it is obvious that the conception of the function of philosophy involves the assumption referred to above. Indeed, that this is the case becomes a matter of definition.

Which analytic philosophers accept this view of the function of philosophy? It is difficult to say. Wittgenstein did not hesitate to make rather sweeping pronouncements about philosophy, even if his actual procedure, when dealing with concrete issues, was not noticeably governed by these pronouncements.[14] Generally speaking however, analytic philosophers are very hesitant to make general statements about philosophy. A good many years ago Gilbert Ryle expressed his somewhat reluctant inclination to believe that philosophical analysis was the sole function of philosophy, and that it takes the form of the 'detection of the sources in linguistic idioms of recurrent misconstructions and absurd theories'.[15] But J.L. Austin carefully refrained from claiming that his way of doing philosophy was the only way. On the contrary, he spoke of it as one possible way of doing what was possibly one part of philosophy. Those critics of analytic philosophy who have decided views of their own about the nature and function of philosophy are understandably inclined to become either perplexed or exasperated when they find themselves unable to elicit from the analysts clear and definite statements of an analogous kind. The fact remains however that any attempt to attribute to the analytic philosophers a set of definite presuppositions or a set of explicit theses about the nature of philosophy is likely to meet with criticism or even downright rejection.[16]

Let us assume however that the actual procedure of some analytic philosophers implies or at any rate suggests the presupposition that, in Wittgenstein's words, 'philosophy simply puts everything before us, and neither explains nor deduces anything',[17] and that 'if one tried to advance theses in philosophy, it would never be possible to debate them, because everyone would agree with them'.[18] I very much doubt whether such dogmatic pronouncements would in fact meet with much agreement nowadays. But, for the sake of argument, let us assume that some would accept them. There are one or two comments which should be made. In the first place, even if the philosopher is unable to make 'discoveries', it does not necessarily follow that the resolution of substantive issues which transcend the sphere of philosophy belongs exclusively to empirical science. For example, let us suppose that while the philosopher can examine and reflect on religious language, including talk about God, he cannot tell us whether the term 'God' has or has not objective reference. It hardly needs saying that empirical science cannot tell us either, not at any rate if 'God' is taken to refer to a transcendent reality. This becomes a matter of faith. And neo-Wittgensteinian philosophy and Barthian theology can therefore co-exist. In the second place, even if one holds that philosophy is mainly concerned with the mapping out of ordinary language, it by no means follows that the philosopher is condemned to silence once science has put its oar in, not at any rate if we understand ordinary language as covering not only the language of Everyman but also the language of science. The philosopher as such cannot indeed discover the physiological basis of our perception of colours or the atomic constitution of material things. But he can try to show how *prima facie* opposed statements are compatible, if, that is to say, he thinks that this is the case. For instance, whereas we are accustomed to speak of things as coloured, ascribing colour to the things, others may claim, on scientific grounds, that this way of speaking is incorrect. A puzzle thus arises, which the philosopher can try to solve in such a way as neither to make nonsense of our ordinary way of speaking nor to deny established scientific facts.

6. Now analysis of language, if it is to be philosophical analysis, obviously involves conceptual analysis. And this activity can take the form of trying to exhibit the basic concepts in terms of which man conceives the world, himself and his environment. This attempt to reveal and elucidate the basic concepts expressed in or implied by ordinary language has been called by Professor P.F. Strawson 'descriptive metaphysics', as distinct from the 'revisionary metaphysics' which aims at changing our view of the world.[19] The enterprise seems to me a perfectly legitimate and worthwhile theoretical activity. But certain questions arise in connection with it. And I wish to draw attention to one or two of them.

In the first place, if we are looking for the basic concepts in terms of which all men see the world, are we assuming that as an empirical fact men in general nowadays share common basic concepts, perhaps through the development of a unified cultural background? Or are we assuming that man necessarily sees the world in certain ways, that human thought as such has a certain conceptual structure?

It is not my intention here to object to either assumption, provided that it is proposed as a working hypothesis and not as *a priori* dogma. The assumptions however are already different, as can be seen by referring to the concept of 'revisionary metaphysics'. If human beings simply happen, as an empirical fact, to see the world in similar ways, it is conceivable that the *de facto* basic conceptual structure should be changed. It is in principle subject to change. If however human beings are thought necessarily to see the world in certain ways, by reason of the very nature of thought, this basic conceptual structure is not subject to change. In this case revisionary metaphysics could affect only what is variable.

One can of course make the questioning rather more complex. For example, if we assume that human beings necessarily see the world in certain similar ways or in terms of similar basic concepts, is this necessity of the kind postulated by Kant, a necessity belonging to the nature of thought itself, so that the fundamental conceptual or categorial structure can be brought to light by the mind's transcendental reflection on its own activity? Or is the necessity one of life, in the sense that man cannot live, that he cannot master phenomena in such a way as to make life possible, unless he employs certain concepts? In other words, is it a case of indispensability for life, as Nietzsche suggested?

In the second place, to what extent do the basic concepts have ontological reference? Are the basic categories of thought also categories of things? If we regard the basic concepts as formed in response to man's experience of the world, it is reasonable to claim that they have some ontological basis, even if other ways of interpreting or grasping phenomena might be possible in principle. If however we regard the basic concepts as *a priori* forms of human thought, their relation to what Kant called the thing-in-itself becomes problematic.

7. One can hardly claim that analytic philosophy gives these or those definite answers to such questions. For one thing there is no homogeneous analytic philosophy, no set of doctrines to which all analytic philosophers subscribe. What is called analytic philosophy is a movement, not a school. For another thing the analytic philosophers, generally speaking, have been more intent on pursuing particular conceptual analyses than with treating the sort of questions which I have raised. It seems however safe to say that so-called linguistic philosophy, by its very nature, does not favour a Kantian point of view. If language has been developed by man in society, in response to his needs, and if there are in fact pervasive concepts which find expression in or are implied by language, it is natural to suppose that they express man's common experience of himself and his environment. Let us assume, for example, that a distinction between persons and things is implied by ordinary language, by, for instance, our use of pronouns, such as 'I', 'he' and 'it'. The verdict of common sense would presumably be that we make this distinction because it is demanded by objective differences between human beings on the one hand and, say, stones and tables on the other. And I imagine that the common-sense view is also that of the ordinary language philosophers, even if they

might possibly leave the topic to psychologists.[20] It might perhaps be objected that there was a time when no clear distinction of the kind mentioned was made. Though however this line of objection would militate against the idea that the concepts of person and thing were *a priori* categories of human thought, it would not necessarily militate against the common-sense view. For the reply could be made that the distinction developed in response to man's growing experience and knowledge of himself and his environment and to his increasing appropriation of this experience, an appropriation which has expressed itself in language. As for the future, it is difficult to see how science could render the distinction otiose or outdated. For the scientific enterprise seems to depend on the existence of persons. Science is their construction. We can say indeed that the distinction is required for life, inasmuch as it is implied by human society. But it is required for life because it reflects the existing state of affairs.

In effect I am suggesting that analytic philosophy has realist presuppositions. To be sure, some qualification is needed. It is arguable, for example, that the ontology which is found at the beginning of Wittgenstein's *Tractatus* was developed *a priori*, in the sense that it depended on his picture-theory of the proposition, being thus a deduction from logic. And though G.E. Moore was and remained a common sense realist, it is not easy to see how some of the things which he said about sense-data can be reconciled with this realism. But the sense-datum theory came under heavy attack from philosophers such as J.L. Austin, and a robust common-sense attitude is characteristic of Gilbert Ryle.

8. Wittgenstein asserted that philosophy 'leaves everything as it is'.[21] He was actually talking about language and maintaining that it was not philosophy's job to interfere with language or change it. It is not surprising however if critics have accused ordinary language philosophy of being conservative, or at any rate neutralist, neutralist in metaphysics, neutralist in ethics, and neutralist in politics. Professor E. Gellner drew attention to this feature of linguistic philosophy in *Words and Things*.[22] And in his work *Marxism and Linguistic Philosophy*[23] Mr Maurice Cornforth wrote that this kind of philosophy is 'on all social questions, in relation to all the problems of real life,

remarkably quietist, non-partisan and non-militant'.[24] It may be appropriate if I make brief remarks about this line of thought.

It is indeed a far cry from the statement that philosophy leaves everything as it is to Marx's demand that philosophers should cooperate in changing the world. Those however who would be prepared to endorse Wittgenstein's statement would emphasize the word 'philosophy'. In answer to the charge that linguistic philosophy comes down heavily on the side of the *status quo* they point out that in their social and political convictions analytical philosophers differ from one another, and that some are by no means conservatives. Where they agree is in the view that philosophy is not competent to settle our outstanding social, political and economic issues. It can clarify the use of language, examine arguments from a logical point of view and contribute to the dissipation of confusion and the promotion of clear thinking. But the philosopher can no more do the work of the politician or the economist for him than he can do the work of the physicist or the biologist. Philosophy may be in a sense neutral; but it by no means follows that philosophers, considered as men and citizens, must be neutral.

This line of reply seems to me reasonable, as far as it goes. There is obviously no good reason for thinking, for example, that a philosopher as such is qualified to solve our economic problems or problems connected with the production and distribution of food. At the same time there is a good deal that philosophers can do even within the general framework of the analytic movement. The solution of some problems requires a technical knowledge of, say, economics which cannot be demanded of the philosopher as such. There are however social problems which possess ethical aspects. And even if we assume that basic judgments of value cannot be proved, the philosopher can none the less make a real contribution to the solution of such problems. For example, if a society professes, generally speaking at least, adherence to certain ideals or judgments of value, the philosopher, trained, as we may suppose, to clear and logical thinking, can point out the implications of these value-judgments in regard to the issue at hand. For even if basic judgments of value cannot be deduced from premises which contain no value-judgment, such judgments, once made, have implications. Again, the philosopher can examine the arguments adduced by either side in a dispute. Whether the problems at issue are 'philosophical problems' does not seem to be a question of great moment. Even if we assume that there are no specifically 'philosophical problems', there is no reason why the philosopher should not be able to contribute to the solution of some outstanding social issues without his having to claim a technical knowledge which he does not, as a philosopher, possess and without his having to involve himself in implicit contradiction of the 'no-*ought*-from-an-*is* thesis, if he happens to accept this thesis.

In point of fact there seems to have been a shift, within the analytic movement, from what may appear to be trivial examples of ethical problems to consideration of more important issues. One defence for selecting trivial examples[25] was that they are especially suited for encouraging dispassionate discussion, and avoiding the introduction or intrusion of emotive attitudes. And there is indeed some point in the defence. But we now find analytic philosophers addressing themselves to problems of more obvious and general importance, such as the relation between the law and morality in sexual behaviour, capital punishment, ethical aspects of racial problems, and so on. It is thus hardly fair to accuse analytic philosophers in general of neglecting the problems of 'real life' or of making no contribution at all to their solution.

9. In this paper I have tried, in an admittedly sketchy manner, to dispel some misconceptions about analytic philosophy. There is of course a great deal else that one might have said. But I have had perforce to confine myself to a few points. In a larger essay one would try to exhibit some of the complexity of the analytic movement. As it is, one may have given the quite erroneous impression that all analytic philosophers are more or less followers of Wittgenstein, whereas in point of fact the neo-Wittgensteinians form a small group, and they often, though not necessarily, tend to use the later ideas of Wittgenstein in support of religious belief.[26] However I have tried to make it clear that in my opinion it is not true to say either that analytic philosophers are concerned 'merely with words' or that they are committed to by-passing all substantive issues in the ethical and socio-political spheres. Perhaps they ought to be, if they all accepted Wittgenstein's statement that philosophy can only 'describe' the actual use of language. But in point of fact few

analytic philosophers feel themselves constrained by any particular dogma about the nature of philosophy. This is indeed one of the features of the analytic movement that tends to perplex or perhaps to exasperate philosophers of other traditions, namely that, since at any rate the passing of dogmatic logical positivism, philosophers of the analytic persuasion have been extremely reluctant to state clear views about the nature of philosophy or to admit definite presuppositions of their own.

10. For my own part, I think that useful work has been done by analytic philosophers. And I think that in some areas an approach to philosophical problems by way of reflection on ordinary language is both legitimate and sensible. Besides, to remind oneself of the expression of human experience through the centuries can be a useful antidote to easy acceptance of one-sided philosophical theories.[27] At the same time I do not think that linguistic analysis, as ordinarily understood, can properly be regarded as constituting the whole of philosophy. For one thing, it seems to me natural for the human mind to seek conceptual mastery over the multiplicity of phenomena, to pursue a process of unification or synthesis. To be sure, this is partly accomplished in the sciences. But one can reasonably look for an overall view which goes beyond the synthesis of the particular services and which tries to humanize the world of science with the ethical and religious dimensions of human consciousness. In other words, it seems to me that the synthesizing activity of philosophers such as Descartes, Kant, Hegel, Bergson, Whitehead, represents an essential and abiding feature of philosophical thought. For another thing, I sympathize to some extent with those who regard analytic philosophy as too 'neutralist' in, say, the socio-political sphere. Obviously, one should not expect of philosophers an expertise in, for example, the field of economics. Nor can one legitimately expect them to solve all our social and political problems for us. But, as I have suggested in this paper, there is a half-way house between claiming knowledge which one does not possess and refusing to contribute to discussion. If a philosopher believes that philosophy has no special field of its own, this is all the more reason for his bringing his training in logical and clear thought to bear on issues which may not be philosophical issues in any strict sense but

which are of great importance to mankind.

In point of fact a movement towards synthesis has shown itself within the analytic tradition itself. I suppose that this was bound to happen. For example, all language-games are played by man. It is all very well to talk about each language-game expressing a form of life, in which one may or may not participate. These forms of life are all forms of human life. Hence sooner or later reflection on language-games is likely to lead on to some form of philosophical anthropology.[28] Where is one going to stop? In the end one will be led into general views about the relationship between man and his environment. It may appear at first sight that by keeping to minute questions of analysis one can make philosophy truly 'scientific'. But, as Gilbert Ryle, for example, remarked a considerable time ago, 'philosophical problems inevitably interlock in all sorts of ways'.[29]

Of future developments I cannot undertake to speak. Philosophy does not pursue an isolated path of its own; it is one of man's cultural activities and is influenced by other factors in the historical and cultural situation. Any prophecis which one might make on the basis of recent trends in academic philosophy might be falsified through the operation of a variety of factors, including extra-philosophical factors.

Notes

[1] Bradley agreed with Hegel that truth is the whole, and he thought of reality as one, the Absolute. Analysis thus seemed to him a process of breaking up a totality into allegedly self-sufficient units. Russell however was a pluralist, and in his more metaphysical moments he thought of analysis as a means of penetrating to the ultimate constituents of reality.

[2] Bradley subjected to analysis a series of concepts, such as substance, space and time. As for Russell, analysis of mind and matter in terms of events (in his period of neutral monism) obviously brought together what others might consider distinct.

[3] To put the matter in another way, I am concerned with the sort of philosophizing which was sharply criticized by Russell and which he caustically described as pre-occupation with the silly things which silly people are accustomed to say.

[4] Any impression that 'ordinary language' means standard English is doubtless due to the fact that the majority of 'linguistic analysts' have written in English and taken their examples from that language.

[5] *The Philosophical Review*, Vol. 62 (1953).

[6] London, Hutchinson, 1949.

[7] *Contemporary Philosophy*, p. 13 (London, revised edition, 1972).

[8] *The Concept of a Person*, p. 23 (London, 1963)

[9] *Philosophical Papers*, p. 130 (Oxford, 1961).

[10] *Philosophical Papers*, p. 133.

[11] Thus it might be claimed that just as the inadequacy of our ordinary way of talking about the movement of the sun in relation to the earth was shown by astronomy rather than by philosophy, so the inadequacy of the language of freedom (if it is in fact inadequate) can only be shown by the researches of physiologists and psychologists.

[12] This would of course be distinct from the logical positivism of the Vienna Circle. For the ordinary language philosophers do not accept the principle of verifiability as a criterion of meaning.

[13] *Philosophical Investigations*, I, section 124.

[14] On this matter one can read the remarks of A.J. Ayer in his Oxford inaugural lecture, *Philosophy and Language*, pp. 23f (Oxford, 1960).

[15] *Logic and Language*, First Series, edited by A.G.N. Flew, p. 36 (Oxford, Blackwell, 1951). The quotation is from Ryle's article *Systematically Misleading Expressions*, which was originally published in the *Proceedings of the Aristotelian Society* for 1931-2.

[16] In his amusing book *Words and Things* (London, 1959) Professor Ernest Gellner maintained that 'Oxford linguistic philosophy' insinuated a view of philosophy without stating it.

[17] *Philosophical Investigations*, I, section 126.

[18] *Ibid.*, section 128.

[19] See *Individuals, An Essay in Descriptive Metaphysics* (London, 1959).

[20] That is to say, the analyst is likely to concentrate on analysis of the concept of, for example, person and not to concern himself with the genesis of the concept. He is likely to look on this as a psychological topic.

[21] *Philosophical Investigations*, I, section 124.

[22] Cf. pp. 223f.

[23] London, 1965.

[24] P. 261.

[25] I refer to such old favourites as the problem arising when I have promised to take a nephew to a cricket match next Saturday and am then confronted by another, and incompatible, call on my time.

[26] I am thinking principally of the neo-Wittgensteinian theory of autonomous language-games, which can prove attractive to those who wish to insist on the complete autonomy of the language of faith. I do not myself agree with the theory of *complete* autonomy; but this is irrelevant to the point which I am concerned to make.

[27] For example, ordinary language militates against identification of the self either simply with some transcendental ego or with the body, in the sense in which I speak of 'my body'.

[28] This was noted, in regard to the language of ethics, by Professor Stuart Hampshire in *Thought and Action* (London, 1959).

[29] See *British Philosophy in the Mid-Century*, edited by C.A. Mace, p. 264 (London, 1957).

CHAPTER VI

THE NATURE OF METAPHYSICS

1. The title of this chapter, 'The Nature of Metaphysics', tends to suggest that I think of myself as about to unveil an essence. But in point of fact I am not competent to do this. And I feel rather inclined to add as a sub-title "Piffle about Piffle". But as this would be tantamount to falling a victim to the more sceptical moments occasioned by a prolonged, even if not very profound, study of the history of philosophy, I choose instead "Some Remarks about Metaphysics".

2. Perhaps I may start in this way. As we are all aware, Wittgenstein remarks in *The Blue Book* that metaphysics exhibits the 'craving for generality' (p. 18). He also says, of course, that the craving for generality is due to a preoccupation with the method of science, and that it leads the philosopher into complete darkness. On these two points I do not agree with him. Apart from the fact that it would be difficult to show that, historically speaking, metaphysics imitated the method of science, inasmuch as metaphysical philosophy preceded the emergence of physical science as we know it, it seems to me that the so-called craving for generality, which I should prefer to call the tendency to unification, is common both to science and to metaphysics simply because it forms an essential phase in the theoretical understanding of a plurality. When faced with a plurality or multiplicity, we try to obtain conceptual mastery over it. And this involves a process of unification, which does not seem to me to need any further justification than is needed by the work of theoretical understanding in general. Hence I cannot agree that the so-called craving for generality, taken by itself, leads the philosopher into complete darkness.

To be sure, what Wittgenstein has to say is understandable enough in the context of his thought. If, for example, we choose to regard philosophy as concerned with the mapping-out of ordinary language, it is clearly arguable that more light is obtained by examining the differences between different types of language than by seeking for a common essence of language which would either prescind from all differences and blur them or, as happened in logical positivism, involve the elevation of one particular type of language into a model language. And there are doubtless many situations in life in which we can be said to be more interested in differentiating than in unifying. But it might also be claimed that we map out the different forms of language precisely in order to get an adequate view of language as a whole. Unification need not mean conflation. In order to unify we have first to know what we are unifying. And this may well involve differentiation. In other words, differentiation and unification, analysis and synthesis, can be complementary rather than antithetical.

Obviously, I am using what Wittgenstein says as a point of departure for reflection rather than as a text for accurate exegesis. But as I have made critical remarks, it is perhaps appropriate to add that for my part I regard even Wittgenstein's exaggerations, or what appear to me to be such, as capable of exercising an illuminative function. Take, for example, the celebrated statement that whatever can be said at all, can be said clearly. If this is understood literally, it seems to me both untrue and dangerous. Dangerous, that is to say, inasmuch as it would tend, if turned into a dogma, to prevent philosophers from trying to express new ideas after which they are groping and which they perhaps are not yet in a position to express clearly. We might just as well say, as I think that Professor Wisdom has said, that it is precisely the business of philosophers to try to say the unsayable. And yet, of course, Wittgenstein's demarcation between the sayable and the unsayable can be most illuminating. There is, for instance, a sense in which we cannot say anything about the metaphysical subject, the complement of 'my world'. For if I talk about the metaphysical subject, Fichte's pure ego; I objectify it; I make it an object *within* the world, whereas, as Wittgenstein says, it is the limit of 'my world'. Yet language can be used as an instrument to facilitate the metaphysical subject's showing itself as the limit of 'my world'.[1]

Similarly, when Wittgenstein says in the paragraph of *The Blue Book* to which I have referred, that 'it can never be our job to reduce anything to anything', he is presumably ruling out reductive analysis, and so phenomenalism. And whatever we may think of this exclusion, it at any rate draws attention to the fact that phenomenalism *is* a species of metaphysics. When I once represented phenomenalism in this light in a Swedish university, I was taken to task by the professor of philosophy. But it is obviously not physical analysis which is in question. Presumably, therefore, it is meta-physical analysis. I am perfectly well aware, of course, that attempts have been made to present phenomenalism as being simply and solely a theory about *language*. But I am inclined to agree with Professor Ayer when he says in his 1960 inaugural lecture at Oxford that though reductive analysis 'has a linguistic aspect in so far as it seeks to show that one sort of expression can perform the office of another, this is the outcome not of any dispassionate study of language but of an *a priori* conception of reality'. Bertrand Russell, of course, never tried to disguise the metaphysical aspect of his reductive analysis as applied to minds and physical objects. And I am happy to find myself in agreement on at least one point with the most celebrated of living British philsophers.

3. To return from what may appear to be a digression to the subject of unification. This may, of course, take the form of what is sometimes called 'descriptive metaphysics'. But this can itself take a variety of forms.

(*i*) In the first place a philosopher may seek to lay bare the basic conceptual structure by which we think the world. This activity would not, of course, count as metaphysics, if metaphysics were conceived, as it sometimes has been, as a study of an alleged being or beings transcending all possible experience. But it corresponds more or less with what Kant regarded as the only legitimate form of metaphysics, in so far as metaphysics can claim to be a science. Whether it corresponds to a greater or lesser degree obviously depends in large measure on whether the philosopher maintains or does not maintain that the conceptual structure is necessary and hence *a priori*. If he does, he can hardly avoid Kant's problem of the thing-in-itself.

(*ii*) In the second place let us suppose that the philosopher views the fundamental conceptual structure by which we think the world not as a structure which we impose, as it were, on the flux of phenomena but as a structure which arises in the apprehension of objective categories. This view of the matter would obviously correspond more or less with a large part of what Aristotle called 'first philosophy'. That is to say, it would correspond with what, since the time of Wolff at any rate, has generally been called 'ontology'.

(*iii*) But we can make a further distinction.

(a) If a philosopher concerns himself with the objective categories of the greatest generality in the sense of categories which are thought to apply to things simply as beings, we can say perhaps that his metaphysics is to this extent independent of the sciences. Psychologically speaking, of course, some sort of scientific view of the world is probably presupposed. And illustrations of the application of the categories may be taken from the sciences. But the metaphysics or ontology would not formally presuppose the sciences.

(b) But a metaphysician may, of course, explicitly presuppose the sciences and seek for a coherent framework of ideas in terms of which the results, so to speak, of the sciences can be coordinated. He can seek for a general conceptual pattern by which the views of the world presented by the different sciences can be unified, and perhaps in virtue of which all the main forms of human experience and activity, moral, religious, aesthetic, can be synthesized. In this case, of course, the resultant general metaphysical theory is hypothetical and no less subject to revision than the hypotheses of the sciences themselves. Further, there is something analogous to verification or testing. For if the conceptual framework is formed predominantly by reflection on, for instance, physics or biology, the philosopher can then examine whether it is of any service for the interpretation of other fields. This sort of metaphysics can be called 'inductive metaphysics'.

4. Now, it scarcely needs saying that we may wish to quarrel with the theses or theories advanced as the result of any of these activities. For there is no guarantee that the work will be well done. Further, several of the activities alluded to have their own peculiar dangers or drawbacks. For example, an ontology which professes to be independent of the sciences runs the risk of exemplifying, or of appearing to exemplify, the description which William James gave of Scholasticism, namely 'common sense rendered pedantic'. A metaphysical system, however, which presupposes the sciences may easily leave its own bases and assumptions unexamined. And any large scale interpretation of reality is only too likely to be the result of a philosopher's having taken one particular aspect of the world or of

human activity and turning it into a key to unlock all doors. The result may provide an interesting and stimulating vision of the world. But it will be one-sided. There is hardly need to draw attention to the historical systems which exemplify this tendency to over-emphasize one aspect of the world.

At the same time it is difficult to see how we could be justified in trying to prohibit any of these activities as enterprises. It seems to me preposterous, for example, to say that a philosopher is not entitled to attempt general descriptive metaphysics. It seems to me perfectly natural that some people should desire to obtain conceptual mastery, as far as this is possible, over all classes of phenomena. We cannot justifiably set limits *a priori* to the work of generalization or unification.

A further remark. None of the activities to which I have alluded so far necessarily involves the postulation of what are sometimes called 'occult entities'. It is perfectly true that inductive metaphysicians have, as a matter of fact, often postulated trans-empirical realities. Bergson and Whitehead are examples. But to say this is to say that inductive metaphysics has often been explanatory as well as descriptive. As the very name suggests, descriptive metaphysics, considered purely in itself, is either the imposing or the discovery of a categorial pattern. It does not involve inferring the existence of any metaphenomenal or trans-empirical being. According to one interpretation of Hegel the Absolute is simply a name for the universe. And Hegelianism consists in the arrangement in a certain teleological pattern or scheme of the data provided by ordinary experience, by the natural sciences and by what the Germans call the *Geisteswissenschaften*. This is indeed an interpretation about which I entertain some doubts. But if it were correct, the Hegelian system would be a signal example of descriptive metaphysics. True, it would be explanatory in the sense that it would give a teleological interpretation of the process of history. But it would not be explanatory in the sense of trying to explain the existence of the world by postulating a being which transcends the world.

5. However, there certainly have been metaphysicians who have inferred the existence of a being or of beings transcending the sphere of the perceptible. Perhaps neutral monism would be a case in point. And it might be argued that though Wittgenstein

explicitly asserted in the *Tractatus* that from the existence of one thing we cannot infer the existence of any other thing, he himself inferred the existence of simple objects as a condition for our language, the descriptive language of the sciences, having an ultimate anchorage in extra-linguistic reality. At the same time when people talk about metaphysicians inferring the existence of a meta-empirical or metaphenomenal being, they are generally thinking of philosophers such as Aquinas, Descartes, Leibniz, Locke and Berkeley, who have inferred the existence of God. And you have probably been reflecting that it is high time that I turned to this subject. After all, whatever people may have said about metaphysics in the past, the more enlightened do not now object on principle to what I have called 'descriptive metaphysics', borrowing Mr Strawson's term, though I have extended its field of application to cover part at least of what Mr Strawson would call 'revisionary metaphysics'. What people object to is *explanatory* metaphysics. And they object to it not so much because statements about a transcendent reality do not satisfy the neopositivist criterion of meaning as because they see no good reason for inferring the existence of any such reality, and because they feel serious doubts about the validity of any metaphysical interference. Hence if metaphysics, as I conceive it, includes explanatory metaphysics or culminates, rather, in explanatory metaphysics, it is my job to say something in defence of this view.

6. There is, it seems to me, a certain continuity between descriptive and explanatory metaphysics. In descriptive metaphysics there is unification of a plurality in terms of categories or of some general pattern. And unification is also operative in explanatory metaphysics, though attention is directed here to the *that* of things, to their existence, rather than to the *how* of things. In other words, in explanatory metaphysics there is a movement of the mind from the Many to the One in the ontological or existential order.

Mention of explanatory metaphysics naturally suggests the idea of the metaphysicians in question seeking an explanation of the existence of the world. And this in turn suggests that they were guilty of logical error. They thought, for instance, that because it makes sense to ask for an explanation (presumably a causal explanation) of any given phenomenon, it therefore makes sense to ask for the explanation of the whole class of phenomena, of what we call the world. In other words, they assumed that because one finite thing depends for its existence on other things, the whole class of finite things depends on some causal agency outside itself. But this is tantamount to committing the fallacy of predicating of a class the attributes of the several members of the class. And this is a logical error. The class of sheep is not itself a sheep. Nor can we legitimately conclude that because each finite thing is contingent, the whole class of finite things is contingent. The objection that the word 'contingent' should be confined to propositions is indeed irrelevant in one sense. For the fact of the matter is that we can give a cash-value to the term when it is used of things. It indicates, for example, that the thing depends on other things, that it is existentially unstable, insecure. But this is not sufficient to get the metaphysicians out of their difficulty. For the real objection against them is not that they make an illegitimate use of the word 'contingent' when they use it of individual things, but rather that they have no right to extend its use from finite things taken separately to the class of finite things as a whole.

We may be inclined to conclude, therefore, that explanatory metaphysics is simply a logical mistake. It may indeed be an example of generalization or unification. But, if so, it simply confirms Wittgenstein's statement that the craving for generality leads the philosopher into complete darkness. If some philosophers are aware of the logical objections against explanatory metaphysics and nevertheless persist in looking for an explanation of the world or cosmos, this is probably due in large measure to the psychological fact that advertence to manifestations of contingency on the part of finite things can produce a general feeling, so to speak, that the cosmos itself is contingent. This feeling is indeed understandable. Some poets have had it. Among philosophers, Schopenhauer says that philosophy begins with wonder at the existence of the world. And even Wittgenstein himself confessed to feeling this wonder. But Wittgenstein at any rate did not think that the feeling can give rise to any intelligible question or problem. And it is clear that any attempt to use this psychological feeling as the basis for explanatory metaphysics leads one into logical errors which ought to be sufficient evidence of the fact that the enterprise is a mistake.

For my own part I do not think that the objection about

predicating of a class the attributes of the several members of the class is necessarily fatal to explanatory metaphysics. For if a philosopher accepts the reductive analysis which reduces the world to a class, he need not necessarily speak of the class as though it were itself a contingent being. He may do so, of course; but it does not appear to me necessary. It is sufficient for him that the reduction of the world to a class leaves us simply with finite things, each one of which is 'contingent' in a determinable sense of the word. Of course, if he proposes to look for an explanation of the world, he must treat the world in some sense as a whole. But he need not interpret it as a closed totality, so to speak. It is sufficient that he should regard it as an open process which can be considered as a world or cosmos. After all, we do generally consider it as such. And it is not necessary that the philosopher should speak of this process or cosmos as '*a* contingent being'. It is the class of contingent beings. And he looks for an explanation.

The objection then arises, of course, that the metaphysician is presupposing that there *is* an explanation, and that he has no right to presuppose this. We assume that individual phenomena have explanations because we find in practice that they do have them. But we have never found that the whole class of phenomena has one. If we look for such an explanation, we simply presuppose from the start, and without any empirical evidence, that there is one. Hence if the explanatory metaphysician escapes from Scylla, the objection that he predicates of a class the attributes of the several members of the class, he falls into Charybdis, the objection that he presupposes the truth of his conclusion.

Well, if we insist that the metaphysician is not entitled to look for an explanation unless he has already found it, we effectively exclude explanatory metaphysics. But I suppose that the metaphysician might retort that this line of argument would also bar all scientific speculation and hypothesis. On empiricist principles at least we find in particular cases that individual events or phenomena have explanations, and we assume, on the basis of our limited experience, that all events or phenomena have their explanations. Such an assumption is necessary for scientific advance. Why, then should the metaphysician not assume in advance, arguing by analogy, that the whole class of phenomena has an explanation? True, he cannot verify this in the way that a scientific hypothesis can be verified, though he might link up explanatory with descriptive metaphysics in such a way as to permit something analogous to verification. Hence explanatory metaphysics can hardly be removed altogether from the realm of the problematical. That is to say, its validity can hardly be placed beyond question. But at least the metaphysician's presupposition can be placed in such a light that it does not appear so irrational as it may appear at first sight.

If the metaphysician wishes to go further than this in justifying his activity, he will have to argue, I think, that reality is intelligible, and that in his opinion the intelligibility of the world means or involves its explicability. Or, rather, he must argue that empirical reality is explicable because it is intelligible. In fact he presupposes intelligibility even if he contents himself with linking up explanatory with descriptive metaphysics in one overall hypothetical scheme or pattern. For he will probably wish to argue that the scheme of ideas which he selects permits us to give a coherent account of the different aspects of the world and of the different forms of human experience. And this seems to presuppose that the world is of such a nature that a coherent account can be given of it. And to presuppose this is to presuppose its intelligibility. But the metaphysician might argue that science too makes a similar presupposition, and that he himself is not unique in doing so.

If the metaphysician wishes to carry his self-justification further, he will probably have to argue with Aquinas that in knowing anything at all the mind implicitly affirms its aptness to understand being, and so the intelligibility of being. For Aquinas, therefore, the intelligibility of the world is not so much a presupposition in the ordinary sense as something which is implicitly affirmed in any cognitive act. In knowing anything we simply recognize that being is intelligible. And this recognition underlies both science and metaphysics.

Needless to say, explanatory metaphysics is scarcely defensible within the framework of, say, logical positivism. If the metaphysician wishes to enter into a dialogue with the logical positivist, he has first to question the assumptions and dogmas of the positivist. This is sufficiently obvious. Once, however, it is admitted that the principle of verification is primarily a means, whether satisfactory or not, of distinguishing between scientific and non-scientific hypotheses, the way lies open to attributing a positive value to metaphysics, an aesthetic value, for example, or an ethically stimulative value. But once we try to think through what is involved in attributing to metaphysics aesthetic or stimulative value, one will have to admit, in my opinion at least, that it cannot be done without recognizing that metaphysical propositions can have meaning. And once this is admitted, the question of truth or falsity arises, the question of cognitive value. And this is, of course, precisely the point at which many people who reject dogmatic neopositivism part company with the metaphysicians. And understandably so. For can we mention any metaphysical propositions which would be commonly regarded as proved truths? This is a notorious difficulty. But could one mention a list of proved philosophical, though non-metaphysical, truths? One could of course, mention a good many common-sense propositions which everyone believes. But do they believe them because of any philosophical reasons advanced in support of them? Or, if it is said to be absurd to imply that anyone *begins* to belive in common-sense propositions for reasons advanced by philosophers, is one's belief in such propositions in any way strengthened by the arguments of philosophers? This is certainly not obviously the case.

In other words, it might be argued that if explanatory metaphysics has become problematical, so has philosophy in general. There certainly does not seem to be any marked agreement about its nature, function and scope. To be sure, one can say that this kind of philosophy delivers the goods, whereas that kind does not. But if this judgment is used for the purpose of excluding the second kind of philosophy, it seems to be or to imply a judgment of value. After all, when Bertrand Russell says that contemporary 'Oxford philosophy' is good for nothing, except perhaps as a slight help to lexicographers, he is not simple stating that as a matter of fact so-called linguistic analysis does not fulfil a function which it does not pretend to fulfil. He is passing a judgment of value. He is, of course, entitled to do so. But the point is that other people are entitled to their own value-judgments. And similar remarks can be made in regard to metaphysics.

7. Now, I have been talking as though explanatory metaphysicians were concerned simply and solely with satisfying their theoretical curiosity, so to speak: that is, as though they were

concerned with an ultimate explanation in the same impersonal spirit in which an astronomer may seek to increase knowledge simply for the sake of increasing knowledge, or, rathei, to find an explanation simply in order to know it. But I do not for a moment suppose that this account of the matter is an adequate account of the spirit in which *all* metaphysicians go about their business, even if some of them do. For it seems pretty clear to me that some of them at least are searching from the start for an existentially unconditioned One, the Absolute. But I must explain what I am getting at.

There can be little doubt, I think, that what has principally stimulated metaphysicians in the search for the Absolute is advertence to features of things, such as ontological dependence and mutability, regarded as manifesting a radical existential insecurity and instability on the part of the finite thing. In other words, in face of a plurality of dependent, conditioned things the movement towards unification takes the form of a search for the unconditioned One, the Absolute.

The candidate which first offers itself for this title is the world itself. Obviously, many people do think of things as happening 'in the world', as though the world were something which contained all individual things and events. But the world can keep this title only if it is inflated into a Super-substance, something more than the sum of its members. And if a metaphysician believes that this inflation of the world into a Super-substance cannot stand up to a process of reductive analysis which reduces the world to a multiplicity of distinct entities and to the relations between them, he is forced to perform the movement of transcendence. That is to say, he is forced to affirm the existence of an Absolute which cannot be identified with the world. The reason is obvious. If under analysis the world dissolves into the very things which the metaphysician set out to unify by relating them to a common Ground of their being, the world cannot be what he is searching for.

Perhaps I had better remark that though in some articles in *The Heythrop Journal* I have myself applied reductive analysis to the idea of the world, I am not at all happy about it. It is easy enough to say that under analysis the world dissolves into a plurality of distinct things. But what counts as a distinct thing? Clearly, on the common-sense level we all take it for granted that there are distinct things, ourselves for example. But

I do not think that I am able to give adequate criteria for the general use of the term. Moreover, being an old-fashioned 'square' I feel powerfully attracted by the picture of the world given by an idealist such as Schelling, that is, as a dynamic evolving unity, rather than as a collection of distinct things. However, I am unable to mention anything which the world possesses over and above things and the contingent relations between them. I do not believe, for example, in a World-Soul. And the physical view of the world as a dynamic evolving unity may be compatible with the metaphysical point of view of a reductive analysis which dissolves the world into things and contingent relations. Hence for the time being at least I am inclined to accept reductive analysis of the concept of the world, though I do so hesitantly and with considerable misgiving.

However, let us take it that reductive analysis of the concept of the world is O.K. or at least plausible. And let us consider the procedure of the metaphysician who finds himself driven by this analysis to perform what I have called the movement of transcendence. On the one hand he gets neatly out of the difficulty that the dependence of one finite thing is adequately accounted for in terms of its dependence on other finite things. For even if A is dependent on B, B on C and so on indefinitely, the world remains a plurality and consequently cannot be the One for which the metaphysician is seeking. On the other hand the metaphysician gets out of this difficulty only by presupposing from the start that there must be a One, in the sense of the Absolute. Why, for instance, if the metaphysician is convinced that the world does not qualify for the title of Absolute, does he think it necessary to perform the movement of transcendence? The answer is clear. Because he assumes from the start that there must be an Absolute.

In this line of metaphysical reflection difficulties about inferring the existence of an Absolute do not arise. And they do not arise because there is no such inference. And there is no such inference because the existence of the Absolute is presupposed from the start. The only point at issue is where the Absolute is to be found. Can it be identified with the world, or can it not? In other words, must we not conclude that metaphysics of this type rests on an initial act of faith, as indeed Bradley explicitly says that it does?

If we pass over cases in which this initial act of faith is simply the result of already existing religious convictions, it can perhaps be explained by the psycho-analysts. They may be able to explain why some people have that deep-seated dissatisfaction with the world as we find it which seems to be characteristic of many metaphysicians. But there is no need to harp on the subject of psycho-analysis. From the purely philosophical point of view the important point is that the metaphysician really presupposes his conclusion from the start. And this is doubtless the reason why he is impervious to such objections as, 'Why are you not content with empirical explanations?' For if he presupposes the existence of a meta-empirical Absolute, whether it is to be identified with the world inflated into a Super-substance or with a transcendent Being, he obviously cannot be content with empirical explanations.

8. This line of objection seems to me not only impressive but also in some sense true. But in what sense?

Terms such as 'presupposition' tend to suggest a free assumption, one that we are free to make or not to make, as when a government first assumes that another government will act in manner X and then that it will act in manner Y, and considers the appropriate measures to be taken in each eventuality. But if the metaphysician assumes the existence of an Absolute in this sense, we are back in hypothetical metaphysics, whereas the type of metaphysics which I am considering is the type which professes to prove the existence of the Absolute not as a more or less probable hypothesis but as a certain truth. And in this case the presupposition must be a necessary presupposition, or the whole edifice of this type of metaphysics collapses.

In point of fact some metaphysicians have tried to show that the Absolute is a necessary presupposition. Bradley, for example, argued that every judgment affirms the Absolute. And a prominent group of modern Thomists seem to have adopted a more or less similar position. For my own part I am inclined to suggest that the existence of an unconditioned One in the ontological order is a postulate of reason itself when operating in a metaphysical context. That is to say, in face of a plurality of things considered as 'contingent' unification takes the form of relating these things to a One in the ontological order. I am aware, of course, that I lay myself open to the objection, in Kantian language, of turning a regulative Idea of unity into a constitutive Idea. But on this subject I am inclined to agree with Kant's successors rather than with Kant himself.

At the same time I do not think that I can defend my point of view in such a manner as to compel anyone else to assent to it. And I frankly admit that I see in metaphysics, that is, in metaphysics of the type under discussion, a profoundly religious significance. That is to say, I see in the movement of the mind towards the Absolute one expression of the orientation of the human spirit to God so that the metaphysics of the Absolute appears to me as the finite spirit's reflection on its own dynamic orientation. If it is said that I lay myself open to the charge of interpreting metaphysics in the light of a certain system or in that of theological presuppositions, I do not know that this worries me very much. For I doubt whether the type of metaphysics which I have in mind can be turned into a completely autonomous deductive system which should compel the assent of anyone who understands the terms used. I am inclined to think that the metaphysics of the Absolute is best seen as a phase in a general process which includes reflection on such themes as the great religions of humanity and religious experience. As for definite theological commitments, these may, of course, be entirely absent. We then have a metaphysics in which the emphasis is placed primarily on openness to the Transcendent, as in the philosophy of Karl Jaspers. If, however, there is a commitment to the idea of a definite response, as it were, on God's part, metaphysics is linked with a theology of revelation.

10. You may have concluded from all this that if I regard metaphysics in general as culminating in the philosophy of the Absolute, metaphysics becomes for me problematic and ambiguous in proportion as it approaches its culminating point, in proportion, one might say, as it grows more 'metaphysical'. But I very much doubt whether metaphysics can ever be placed beyond the sphere of controversy. For one thing, the philosophy of the Absolute involves us in talking about themes for which our language is not really fitted. For example, in the course of this chapter I have referred to a transcendent Absolute. But the use of the word 'transcendent' immediately suggests spatial distance. And though one may explain that one means by transcendence in this context not spatial separation but the

non-identifiability of the Absolute with its self-manifestations, directly one tries to give precise expression to the relation between the Infinite and the finite, one will find oneself in difficulties. It may appear, therefore, that the correct policy is one of silence. But though silence may be golden, speech may be natural, even if it leaves metaphysics in the sphere of the problematic. In my opinion at least it will remain there. For I believe that the recurrent waves of metaphysics and of anti-metaphysics reflect distinguishable aspects of the nature of man. And if man were radically different from what he is, he would presumably not be man.

CHAPTER VII

MARX AND HISTORY

1. Karl Marx died in 1883. In a note to *Ludwig Feuerbach and the End of Classical German Philosophy* (1885) Friedrich Engels generously attributed to his dead friend the lion's share in formulating the materialist conception of history. 'Marx', he says, 'was a genius; we others were at best talented'. In the following remarks I shall confine my attention to Marx, with some references to Engels. I am not concerned with Marxism-Leninism, nor with the ideas of the late Chairman Mao.

On the monument to Marx in the cemetery at Highgate in London there stands the famous statement (taken from the *Theses on Feuerbach*) that whereas philosophers had hitherto only interpreted the world, the point was to change it. As we are all aware, Marx was committed to the cause of revolution and to the creation of what he regarded as a truly human society, in which class antagonism, exploitation and war would be overcome. When in *The Communist Manifesto* Marx and Engels said that the fall of the bourgeoisie and the victory of the proletariat were 'equally inevitable', they doubtless meant what they said. But they were not speaking about something which they regarded as inevitable but towards which they felt indifferent. They regarded the victory of the proletariat and, as they somewhat optimistically hoped, the advent of a better society as something desirable, something for the speedier realization of which they were prepared to work.[1]

Precisely however because Marx was a committed revolutionary and a man who obviously made or implied judgments of value, there is a danger of thinking of him as a pragmatist who proposed those theoretical ideas which he thought were most likely to work, to contribute to the realization of the desired goal. A view of this kind would be a caricature. When Marx said that philosophers had only interpreted the world in various ways, he was not blaming them for trying to interpret it. The operative word was 'only'. He was doubtless thinking largely of Hegel, who had said that no philosophy can transcend its own time and who had left the future to look after itself, so to speak, apart from a few more or less common-sense prophecies,

131

such as that America was the land of the future. Hegel looked backwards, thinking of his philosophy as the highest expression of the self-consciousness of the human spirit up to date. Marx looked backwards and forwards. He looked backwards not simply to interpret the past but also to be able to contribute intelligently to the future of mankind. But in order to be able to do this, it was essential, in his judgment, to have a genuine knowledge of history, of what was basic and of what was secondary or derived, of the laws of social change. It was thus not the mere fact that philosophers had tried to interpret the world and human history which excited Marx's disapproval. There were two reasons for his disapproval. One has been mentioned, namely that the philosophers did not understand the union of theory and practice, that ideas are the first stage of action. The other reason is that the philosophers, such as Hegel, had, in Marx's opinion, *mis*interpreted human history. They had got things upside down. For Hegel, history was the progressive self-manifestation of the Absolute as Spirit. For Marx, history was the work of man in his dialectical relationships with nature and with his fellows. In other words, Marx wanted to establish the true interpretation of human history, not simply a pragmatically useful one. More precisely, the true interpretation, the science of history, would be the useful one.

2. In the manuscript of *The German Ideology*, written by Marx and Engels in 1845-46, it is said that history can be looked at under two aspects, the history of nature and the history of man. These two are not completely independent. For human beings live by acting on nature, while nature acts on human beings. The relationship is dialectical. None the less, says Marx, the history of nature can be excluded from present consideration.

This passage was crossed out and did not appear in the published version of *The German Ideology*. I do not know the reason for this. But one possible reason which occurs to me is that Marx may have seen the questionable implication of the statement that there is only one science, the science of history. The statement implies that physics, if it is a science (as Marx certainly believed it to be), could properly be included under the label of history. And this is clearly questionable.[2]

Mention of 'a science' of history however clearly indicates Marx's attitude. If man is confronted by a nature, a physical environment, of which he is entirely ignorant, he is at the mercy of nature. The practical possibility of control grows in proportion to our scientific knowledge of nature and of what we call its laws. Control of nature is obviously limited, but the basis of intelligent control is scientific knowledge. Magic is no substitute. Similarly, it is human beings who make their history; but they can do so intelligently only if they know the laws of social development, the laws of history. Just as we cannot fly to Mars if we disregard or try to flout natural laws, so we cannot create the sort of society which we desire if we disregard or try to flout the laws of social development. In both cases intelligent and fruitful action presupposes knowledge. And Marx certainly thought of himself as making a contribution to the science of history in general, even if he came to concentrate more and more on analysis of the contemporary western industrialized society in which he lived.

This point of view obviously assumes that there can be a science of history. And this is a matter which is open to discussion. It is not a question of whether there can be more or less objective historiography in the ordinary sense, whether there can be degrees of objectivity in historical writing. In practice we all assume that there can be, even if philosophers of history propose and discuss puzzles relating to the possibility of objectivity in history. It is a question of historical laws. Historians tell intelligible connected stories, but they rarely appeal to laws to explain events, though they may of course report the formulation of laws, Boyle's law for example. A science of history is not the same thing as historiography. And the question whether there can be such a thing as the science of history, parallel to physical science, is at any rate open to discussion. But we can hardly discuss the question here. Marx clearly assumes that there can be such a thing. And if he were alive today, he might well sympathize with what is called the covering law theory of historical explanation.

The concept of a science of history has a bearing on the problem of freedom in Marx's thought. In chapter eleven of *Anti-Dühring* Engels (who read the manuscript to Marx and received his approval) asserts that freedom consists in the knowledge of laws and in the possibility, conferred by this knowledge, of using them to attain definite ends. If we know the laws of nature, we can use them to attain our ends. Similarly, if we know the laws of history, we can make use of them in creating the sort of society we want. I do not say that this solves the problem of freedom in Marxism. For Marx certainly speaks as though the coming of Communism were inevitable, whatever human beings may wish and do. But I suppose that this confidence in the coming of Communism was based in large measure on Marx's analysis of the capitalist economy, which he regarded as developing in such a way as to bring about a situation in which the transition to socialism would be inevitable sooner or later. People who understood the situation could accelerate or retard this transition, even if they could not prevent it altogether. This was part of Marx's general thesis that though it is human beings who make history, they are always faced by a given situation which, while creating possibilities for action, also limits these possibilities.

3. Marx never actually wrote any extended treatment of the materialist conception of history. Apart from some study of what he called the Asiatic mode of production,[3] he devoted his attention mainly to a critical analysis of capitalist society. However, Marx and Engels together give us a statement of the basic principles of their interpretation of history and an outline or sketch of the theory. The main lines are familiar. The basic and primary factor in human history is man's economic life, without which there would be no political life, no law, no cultural activities, such as art and philosophy. To have any cultural life at all, man must sustain himself physically. He does so by his labour, by producing the means of subsistence. His labour, his working in some way on nature, is not however simply an individual act. Human beings in the productive process determine the forms of society. Division of labour in the productive process leads in the end to property relations and to the emergence of classes. Apart from the family, the economic class is the basic form of society, the State, when it arises, being an organ of the dominant class. The productive relations however are not static. They change, especially when human beings discover new means of production. And social forms change with them. It is this economic life of mankind which lies at the basis of human history. Man's cultural life, his morality, his art, his religion and so on belong to a superstructure which presupposes the economic basis, is ultimately dependent on it and changes with it.

Hegel believed that the dialectic of national States, or of national spirits, was the basic factor in the historical process. For Marx, this was a superficial view. The economic class was more fundamental than the State. History, for him, was characterized by the dialectic of economic classes, a dialectic which must needs continue until the forces of production have been developed to such an extent that transition to a classless society, a truly human society, becomes possible. To achieve this development of the productive forces is the historical mission, so to speak, of the bourgeoisie. In the process however a situation emerges which the capitalist class is unable to control, and which demands a transcending of capitalist society. The bourgeoisie, one may say, serves the cause of humanity, but, in doing so, it digs its own grave as a class. As however no dominant class surrenders its power voluntarily, a revolution of some sort is inevitable, though not necessarily a bloody one.[4]

It is not possible to do more than make a few remarks about this inadequate sketch of Marx's view of history. In the first place some statements made by Marx and Engels seem to be truisms. For example, it is hardly startling news that there could be no cultural life, unless human beings kept themselves alive by eating and drinking and providing shelter for themselves. Such statements however have to be seen in the context of Marx's critique of German idealist philosophy. Marx and Engels may have tended to caricature the German philosophers. But they thought of the philosophers as conceiving thought and its products as primary and neglecting the vulgar fact that man's biological needs are basic. The German thinkers had to be brought back to earth.

In the second place, I suppose that everyone nowadays would be prepared to admit — largely, no doubt, under the influence of Marx himself — that economic life can affect political forms, the law, even morals and religion in a variety of ways. There is no need to make a song and dance about this. We can all think of examples. The ferocious penalties attached to petty stealing in the early part of the nineteenth century in England clearly reflected the interests of the propertied class or classes. There is no need to multiply illustrations.

In the third place, we must make a distinction between claiming simply that economic life can affect other elements in human civilization and claiming that economic life is the infrastructure which determines the superstructure and is reflected in it. In regard however to economic determinism Marx's view can easily be exaggerated. Writing after Marx's death, Engels admitted that in order to make their point Marx and himself had had to emphasize the role of economic life in such a way as to give the impression that in their view economic life was the only active causal agent in human history, all else being a passive reflection of economic conditions. This was not however what they really meant. For one thing, elements in the superstructure, religious beliefs for example, could certainly exercise an influence on other elements. For another thing, the materialist conception of history should not be taken as implying that economic life is the only relevant factor in determining forms of political society and of our cultural life. In a letter to Joseph Bloch (1890) Engels said, 'according to the materialist conception of history, the *ultimately* determining element in history is the production and reproduction of life. More than this neither Marx nor I has ever asserted'. To say that economic life is the 'ultimately' determining element is to make a rather vague statement. Engels' point however is that the ways in which economic life determines the superstructure and the ways in which one component of the superstructure influences another component or even reacts on economic life cannot be known *a priori* but are matters for historical inquiry. One may add that the traditional division of historical periods (Asiatic, ancient or Greco-Roman, feudal, and bourgeois or capitalist) should not be regarded as sacrosanct. It would be possible, within the framework of Marx's thought, to make a different classification of periods, provided of course that one adhered to the basic principles, especially that of the priority and ultimately determining influence of economic life.

What I am getting at is this. From one point of view Marx's interpretation of history can be regarded as an empirical hypothesis, a heuristic theory. To put the matter in another way, Marx might be regarded as offering a programme for research. On the assumption that economic life is the ultimately determining factor in human history, we could then reflect on history as represented by historians with a view to ascertaining to what extent the assumption or hypothesis was empirically confirmed. There is of course the danger that those facts will be selected for emphasis which tend to support the hypothesis and that recalcitrant facts will be slurred over, explained away, or even passed over altogether. The hypothesis then tends to become an unquestionable dogma. But it is not necessary to treat it in this way. One might be prepared to abandon it, if one found that it was insufficiently confirmed.

It is not my intention to suggest that the truth or falsity of Marx's materialism can be settled in this way. There are philosophical problems to which Marx pays scant attention. He pretty well assumes that Feuerbach was right in rejecting the ontological priority of Spirit, and he proceeds on this assumption. All that I am suggesting is that the economic theory of history can be treated as a working hypothesis rather than as a dogma which is beyond question. And it is possible for a university teacher to treat it in this way, without committing himself to supporting, for example, the policies of the Kremlin. This has not always been properly understood, though it ought to have been.[5]

4. There is however another side to Marx's thought. On the one hand he insisted that it is human beings who make history, and that History, with a capital letter, accomplishes nothing. In the *Theses on Feuerbach* he criticized the view of some materialists that human beings are simply the products of their circumstances or environment. Materialists of this kind forget that it is human beings who change circumstances. To be sure, their power of action is limited. Medieval man could not fly to the moon. Nor could modern industrialized society be created at will in ancient Athens. But this does not mean that human beings are unable to affect their environment, physical or social, in any way. On the other hand, Marx was, as we have reminded ourselves, a committed revolutionary; and it is not unreasonable to claim that he wanted to feel that history was, so to speak, on his side, and that history was moving inevitably towards a goal, the classless society in which all would be truly free. It is in this context that Marx's so-called Messianism comes to the fore; and it is in this context that the problem of freedom becomes acute. Marx allows indeed for human beings accelerating or retarding the process, but he seems unable to allow for the possibility of history taking a different path from that which he expected.

Perhaps the matter can be put in another way. Marx envisaged the establishment of a science of history, as an instrument for action. Nowadays we do not think of science as something finished and complete and definitive. Scientific theories are subject to possible revision, and general theoretical frameworks of reference can change. This way of looking at science should apply also to a science of history, if such a thing is possible. But when what Sir Raymond Firth has called 'gut-Marxism', as distinct from 'cerebral Marxism', gets the upper hand, flexibility is diminished. Something analogous to religious faith takes over. And there are at any rate some signs of this in Marx's theory of history.

5. It seems to me therefore that Marx's conception of human history has two aspects. On the one hand it can be seen as a teleological view of history, a view of the historical process as moving towards a goal.[6] This involves a totalization of human history, in the sense that the histories of various peoples are seen as converging towards a common end. Marx thought of the most highly industrialized nations as forming the spearhead or advance guard, but he conceived other nations too as being caught up by and carried along with the movement. Again, though there is no compelling reason to suppose that Marx thought of an ideal society being achieved overnight, he certainly thought its advent presupposed human history up to date. In his view, mankind has to pass through successive stages to reach the goal. In this sense too the historical process could be regarded as a unity, though a complex one of course. For Marx however, there was no divine providence to ensure the victory of the City of Jerusalem, as in St Augustine's theology of history. Nor was there any absolute spirit which progressively manifested itself in history, as in the philosophy of Hegel. The dialectic and its laws had to take the place of the Absolute. But this was a subject to which Engels paid more attention than Marx did, though there does not seem to be any good reason for asserting that Marx disapproved of Engels' theories.[7]

This totalizing view of human history as a teleological process can fairly be called a philosophy of history. It can exercise a powerful appeal on those who are acutely conscious of injustices and shortcomings in present-day society and who desire a society of the kind envisaged by Marx. The fact that Marx spoke of the society of the future in pretty general terms and did not attempt to provide a complete blueprint of what did not yet exist probably renders the appeal all the greater. In any case the Marxian conception of history as a dialectical goal-directed process has seemed to a considerable number of people to provide a sound basis for confidence that history is, so to speak, on their side. To my mind, the only sound basis for confidence in the coming of a better society would be a common will to create one, accompanied by basic agreement on what would constitute a better society. In other words, I endorse the dictum of Karl Marx that it is human beings who make history, though the possibilities of action are always limited by the situations in which human beings find themselves at any given time. One can however easily understand the appeal of the picture of history as a teleological process which inevitably works itself out through the actions of human beings.

On the other hand, it is possible to disregard the aspect just mentioned, to lay emphasis on Marx's analysis of the society in which he was living, and to regard him more as a social scientist than as a speculative philosopher. Indeed, it is possible to see him as trying to overcome, so to speak, speculative philosophy of history and to establish a science of history, or at any rate a scientific approach to history. The question arises of course whether there can be such a thing as a science of history. This seems to me a difficult question to answer. For one thing, it is difficult to identify precise criteria for distinguishing between general statements which can properly count as laws and those which cannot properly be described in this way. None the less, there is no good reason why someone should not attempt to develop a science of history, based on the assumption or hypothesis that economic life is the ultimately determining factory in human history. It is indeed regrettable if the hypothesis is converted into a dogma or presented as a scientific truth which is so certain that it cannot be called in question.[8] For this attitude inhibits free inquiry. But Marx and his followers are also free to entertain their hypothesis and to explore and test its applications.

Furthermore, if today historians pay a great deal more attention than was once the practice to the economic life of human beings and to its influence on other factors, this is largely due, I think, to Karl Marx. There have indeed been other writers who have emphasized the importance of economic life; but it is Marx who has really struck people's imagination. This may obviously be due in large part to his association with a powerful social-political movement and Party, which can hardly be ignored, whatever our opinions of it may be. But it is also due, in my judgment, to the forcible way in which Marx presents his theory. For my own part, I am inclined to mistrust assertions that this or that particular factor is the ultimately determining factor in human history. At the same time the mere fact of identifying and emphasizing one particular factor in this way forcibly directs attention to it and makes us see what we perhaps had not seen before. We need not be Freudians in order to be able to admit that after Freud psychology has not been the same as it was before him. Freud made a difference, as we say, extravagant as some of his speculations may have been. So has Marx made a difference, a big difference, not only by the practical effects of his doctrine but also in regard to the understanding of human history and of society. We do not need to be Marxists, still less do we need to be Communists, in order to recognize this.

6. An aspect of Marx's philosophy of history on which I have hardly touched is the humanistic aspect. Those Marxist thinkers who are sometimes described as revisionists have been inclined to make a distinction between dialectical materialism on the one hand, with its emphasis on class-man and on the class war, and, on the other hand, the genuine thought of Marx himself, which they have represented as much more humanistic than what passes for orthodox Marxism in Party circles. For evidence of Marx's humanism they have tended to appeal to early writings in which Marx refers to the overcoming of alienation in mankind in general and understands alienation, which appears in the course of history, in a pretty general sense, not being confined to strictly economic alienation.

Against this point of view it has been argued that the early manuscripts in question show Marx in the process of emerging from idealist philosophy, and that they do not represent his mature thought. Further, neither Marx nor Engels (after Marx's death) thought it worth while publishing the early manuscripts and regarded them as best forgotten. Marx progressively freed himself from Hegelian influence, and in so far as he retained the concept of alienation, he understood it in purely objective terms, as clearly definable economic alienation. There is no good reason therefore for seeing a clash between Marx the humanist and a dialectical materialism which is alleged to have abandoned or glossed over the humanist element in Marx's thought. To appeal to the early writings to justify this antithesis is equivalent, as it has been put, to appealing to material from Marx's own wastepaper basket.

It is doubtless true that Marx moved progressively further away from philosophy, that he came to concentrate his attention on the analysis of capitalist or bourgeois society, and that he came to think of alienation in economic terms. At the same time there seems to me to be a sense in which Marx always remained a humanist. Thus he looked beyond the era of class war to the birth and development of a society in which man would be fully man, rather than class-man. Even in *Capital* (1, ch. 13) he refers to the 'totally developed individual'. The question obviously arises whether Marx's view of man is adequate. He did not indeed regard human nature as static, but rather as changing by developing fresh needs. But are man's needs simply those recognized by Marx? For example, is religion simply what Marx says that it is? These are questions which cannot be discussed in this short talk. My point is that there is a real sense in which Marx's thought always retained a humanist element. It is the vision of a truly human society as the goal of history which has obviously exercised a powerful influence on the minds of more idealistically motivated adherents of Marxism. For my own part, I am inclined to lay emphasis on Marx's rôle as representing a transition between speculative philosophy of history and social science. But I am well aware that this point of view is apt to seem academic and dry as dust.

Notes

1 On the one hand Marx regarded the transformation of capitalist society as inevitable, in the sense that capitalism develops the productive forces to such an extent that it is increasingly unable to control them, and that it creates and develops in its midst the instrument of change, namely the proletariat. On the other hand he obviously welcomed the prospect of this transformation, thus making or implying a judgment of value. The two attitudes are doubtless compatible, but they ought to be distinguished. For one might regard something as inevitable and yet feel indifferent towards it.

2 Physical science obviously has a history, the story of its development. But physics as taught at any given time is not yet history. Consider chemistry. Chemistry as now taught belongs in a sense to the history of chemistry, in the sense that it is a phase in

the historical development of chemistry. But a great deal of information is relevant to the history of chemistry which is irrelevant to the teaching of chemistry as a science. We must make some distinction.

3 Marx was thinking, for example, of ancient India. He argued that while land was held in common and villages were uninterested in external affairs, agriculture depended on irrigation, which in turn was dependent on the resources of the State, of a central government. In developing his idea of the Asiatic mode of production he used ideas derived from English writers. At the same time we might perhaps see in Marx's concept of this historical stage an economic interpretation of Hegel's idea of oriental despotism.

4 Marx envisages the proletariat becoming so large in highly industrialized countries (with small capitalists, ruined by the growth of large-scale firms and monopolies, relapsing into its ranks) that society would be ripe for a change, for a seizure of political power by the proletariat. To be sure, this move might and most probably would meet with resistance. But not necessarily such that civil war resulted, or that quantities of blood had to be shed. When speaking in Holland, Marx admitted the possibility at any rate of a bloodless revolution. One can add that when attributing the destruction of native industry in India to Great Britain, he described this destruction as 'revolutionary'. The word, as here used, had obviously no necessary connection with a policy of massacring people.

5 What I mean is of course that it is quite possible to adopt the materialist or economic conception of history as a guiding theoretical framework or as a heuristic hypothesis without supporting the policies of any given State in which a Communist Party exercises political power. For example, it is certainly not logically necessary that a Marxist, in the sense of one who accepts Marx's interpretation of history, should endorse the policies of the Kremlin or of Peking.

6 It should be evident that when I refer here to a teleological view of history, I am thinking of the view that history is a process governed by final causality, in the sense that history moves towards an end or goal which is fixed antecedently to or independently of human choice and in the realization of which human beings serve as instruments, whether or not they are aware of the fact. It seems to me that this sort of view implies theological or metaphysical presuppositions of a kind which have no place in a materialist philosophy. If however we understand by a teleological view of history the idea that history has been moving, purely as a matter of empirical fact, in a certain direction, this view being accompanied by a value-judgment, expressed in an attitude of approval or welcoming of this movement, I have no wish to claim that a materialist is debarred from adhering to such a view.

7 It has sometimes been said that the idea of a dialectic operating in nature was due to Engels and not to Marx, with the implication that the idea was alien to Marx's hand. Though however it was Engels who wrote about the dialectics of nature, there does not seem to be any solid evidence that Marx disassociated himself from Engels' view.

8 It is particularly undesirable that a 'dogma', regarded as sacrosanct, should be passed off as a scientific discovery or as the only possible scientific theory.

CHAPTER VIII

PETER WUST: CHRISTIAN AND PHILOSOPHER

I first met Peter Wust in the autumn of 1938. He was then professor of philosophy in the university of Münster in Westphalia.
A friend had provided me with an introduction, and I went to
call on him at his house. Knowing that he was a professor of
philosophy and having heard of him as a 'profound thinker', I
feared the worst: that is to say, I had thought out some questions about modern German thought, to give myself an excuse
for my visit and him a starting-point for a learned disquisition.
What happened reminded me of the case of the student who
visited Hegel at Berlin and instead of the profound discourse
which he expected was treated to a lively account of the great
philosopher's last trip abroad. Wust, if I remember right, started
talking almost immediately about the political situation and
gave me his frank opinion about the Nazis and about their
policy, both internal and external. After he had been talking for
some time he hesitated, and I saw a look of alarm cross his face.
The cause of his concern was, of course, clear to me, and when
he pointed out that he could be put to death for what he had
been saying, I assured him that I quite understood the situation
and the need for discretion. During the months that I passed in
Münster I frequently heard from his lip trenchant comments
on the exploits of the men who ruled the Third Reich. Possibly
some people, sitting comfortably in their armchairs outside
Germany, might have suggested that Wust ought to have de-
nounced the Nazis from his professorial chair, in the way that
Von Galen, bishop of Münster, did not hesitate to do from the
pulpit. But what would have been gained? Wust would have
been sent to a concentration camp at the very least, and his
family might well have been reduced to destitution. As it was,
he did a great deal more good by expounding in his lectures and
books a philosophy which was incompatible with the Nazi
ideology.

It was at half-past ten, I think, after his morning lecture,
which was given at eight, that Wust was accustomed to leave his
house to walk to the small village of Mecklenbeck where he
drank coffee and discussed philosophical problems, or simply

143

chatted, with his friend Dr Vorholt, until it was time for him to return to Münster for lunch. These walks and discussions formed his recreation, and I was sometimes able to accompany him. It took me a very short time to realize the essential simplicity and directness of the philosopher's outlook. I do not mean by this that his philosophic reflections were superficial; far from it; I mean that sophistication, artificiality and guile were entirely foreign to his character. It always gave me pleasure, and also caused me a twinge of envy, to hear the natural way in which he talked with the children from the farms that we passed on the way. In the lecture-hall he spoke as a man with a message, but in ordinary intercourse he gave a curious impression of childlikeness. No doubt, this quality can be associated with his origins and upbringing; but it was a quality which he retained to the end.

Wust was born at Rissenthal, a small village of some 300 inhabitants in the Saarland, in 1884. His father was a sieve-maker. We must not imagine a factory or workshop. The elder Wust constructed home-made sieves and then went round the neighbouring villages selling them. It was taken for granted that his eldest son, Peter, would one day follow his father's profession, and already at the age of ten he accompanied his father on some of these journeys in the locality. In his memoirs of his early days (*Gestalten und Gedanken*) the philosopher has left us a vivid picture of his father, a deeply religious man but at the same time a romantic, in love with the wandering life of a peddler and never quite able to accommodate himself to a world which did not quite square with his dreams and fantasies. But more striking perhaps is the picture of his maternal grandfather, an old man sitting behind the stove and discoursing on world-history or rather on the philosophy (perhaps better theology) of world-history. In biblical language he announced the fall of the sceptical, rationalist and superficial civilization of his time. Or we catch glimpses of Wust's mother, also deeply religious, yet more practical than his father, or of an aunt, elusive and remote in her profound inner life, yet at the same time simple and natural, devoid of all artificiality and Pharisaism.

It is tempting, though profitless, to wonder what would have happened to the future philosopher, had he remained, as he might so easily have remained, a member of the simple village community in western Germany. Given his intense longing to study and his contemplative and possibly somewhat melancholic temperament, disaster might well have occurred. I remember him telling me about one of the peasant community, who also was a natural philosopher, in the sense that he was naturally given to meditation on the problems of human existence and of human history, and who eventually in his loneliness, in the absence of opportunities for 'communication' and in the lack of stimulus and encouragement through books, took his own life.

The education provided in the village school was naturally rudimentary, and as a small boy Wust was possessed by an insatiable longing for books. When he was about twelve he made a novena to the Child Jesus to obtain books through divine agency. Nothing happened. Undaunted, he made a second novena. And to his delight the schoolmaster lent him a book of his own, containing stories about the Greeks and Romans. Soon after the boy conceived another plan for satisfying his heart's desire. He obtained a large piece of fine paper and wrote to the German emperor. The only result of this move was that his father was summoned to the presence of a local official, at the instance of a marshal of the Court, and told that he ought to discourage his son from addressing such requests to the emperor. The poor boy saw the hour approaching when he would have to leave the *Volksschule* and devote himself to sieve-making and to work on the land. He tells us that he was torn between two desires, his longing for study and his desire to be 'normal', to be like the other children who were only too eager to finish with their lessons and to take to the land or to wander into the town to find work in a factory.

It was the parish priest who came to his rescue. The boy had summoned up courage to approach this somewhat choleric man, and had met with what seemed to him a sharp rebuff. But the priest, whom Wust calls 'the greatest benefactor of my life', had a far kinder heart than his exterior showed, and shortly after Wust had left the elementary school the priest sent for his father and told him that he had decided to give the boy free instruction. Thus from 1898 to 1900 Wust received regular instruction and coaching in Latin from the priest, who then sent him to Trier to sit for the entrance examination of the Friedrich-Wilhelm-Gymnasium. Wust passed the examination and studied at the school from 1900 until 1907.

It was taken for granted that the peasant boy who wanted to

study would become a priest, especially as he came of a deeply religious family; and for some years he resided in a kind of episcopal seminary or hostel, while going daily to the school for classes. As time went on, however, the boy drifted away from the Church and lost his faith, adopting instead an idealistic humanism, largely under the influence of one of his schoolmasters. In 1905 he left the seminary where he resided and took a lodging in the town, supporting himself during his last two years at school by giving tuition. When he matriculated in 1907 all idea of the priesthood had been finally given up. His father tended to look on him as a lost son, and for some time he spent his holidays with his grandparents at Püttlingen.

In 1907 Wust went to the university of Berlin, where Friedrich Paulsen awakened his enthusiasm for philosophy. And so began a third tension in his life. The first tension had been between his passionate desire for study and his apparent destiny to be a maker of sieves and work on a farm. That tension was over and done with. The second was between the faith of his childhood and what he calls 'reflection'. This tension was not to be resolved for some years. The third tension was between his philological studies, which were necessary for practical purposes, and his newly awakened enthusiasm for philosophy. This tension was not finally to disappear until his appointment as professor of philosophy at Münster in 1930.

In 1908 Wust changed to the university of Strasbourg, where he attended lectures on mediaeval philosophy by Klemens Bäumker; and in July 1910 he passed the examination *pro facultate docendi*. In the autumn of the same year he started to teach German and English in a school in Berlin, only to change to Neuss on the Rhine in 1911 and to Trier in 1915, where he was back again, this time as a teacher, in the Friedrich-Wilhelm-Gymnasium. It was during this period at Trier that he had an important conversation with the celebrated philosopher of religion, Ernst Troeltsch. Troeltsch tried to reawaken Wust's faith. Referring to the catastrophe that was then overtaking Germany, he said: 'The external defeat which we are now experiencing need not make you despair. For this external defeat is simply the consequence of the internal defeat which we have already been undergoing since the death of Hegel, inasmuch as we have given up the old faith of our fathers in the sovereign power of the spirit'. This interview with Troeltsch had a considerable influence on Wust, and the following years saw his gradual return to the Church which was completed at Easter 1923. 'From that day I have had again the naive faith of a child'. And at the time I knew him his childlike faith was one of his chief characteristics. When I say that it was childlike, I mean that it was in no way forced or obtrusive. From the point of view of an observer it was not something added to the man, over and above or even contrary to his personality: it was part of the man himself. And it remained so to the end. Obviously enough, I was not in Germany when he died of cancer in 1940: but it has been said of him that he died like a saint. And I can well believe it.

To return, however, to the days of his schoolmastering. I have already mentioned the awakening of Wust's interest in philosophy while he was studying at the university of Berlin. In 1910 he went to Bonn and arranged with Professor Oswald Külpe to write a dissertation on the logical basis of the humanistic sciences in J.S. Mill. This was not perhaps a very promising subject, but it enabled Wust to obtain the title of Doctor on presenting the dissertation in 1914. He was at this time under the influence of Neo-Kantianism, though he never felt really at home in this line of thought. He soon turned to metaphysics, and in 1920 he published *Die Auferstehung der Metaphysik* 'The Reawakening (or Resurrection) of Metaphysics'. He tells us that this work was condemned by the Neo-Kantians, though the younger generation saw in it a liberation from the previously dominant trend of thought.

The metaphysics which came to absorb Wust's attention was the metaphysics of spirit or mind. And the feature of mind or spirit which particularly captivated his attention was 'the restlessness of the heart' (*Die Unruhe des Herzens*) or the principle of oscillation in the human soul. On the one hand the human mind or spirit longs for rest and happiness, in, for example, the possession of truth. On the other hand it is a characteristic of the human mind or spirit not to be content with limits and bounds, but to follow an impulse of restless striving. We can see this in the history of philosophy, for example, where we find the desire to possess the truth coupled with the feeling that any statement of the truth or supposed truth is a limit to be overpassed, a barrier to be surmounted. We can see it too in the individual: − at least we can see it in some individuals, and Wust was one of them. His struggle with the problem of the 'restlessness of the heart' was a struggle with his own problem: the dialectic of the spirit which he discerned in history was something with which he was acquainted in his own inner life. Indeed, his philosophy was so closely connected with his own inner life that we could call him an existentialist philosopher, were it not for the associations which this term has now acquired.

This connection between his philosophy and his own inner life can be seen clearly in the book entitled *Naivität und Pietät* (*Naivety and Piety*), which he published in 1925. He was then a teacher at Cologne, where he had been transferred from Trier in 1921. This period of his life was of considerable importance, because of the friendship which he enjoyed at Cologne with the philosopher Max Scheler. 'For the first time', says Wust, 'I was conscious of meeting intellectual genius'; and he emphasizes the influence of Scheler on his mind. My knowledge of Scheler's philosophy is extremely superficial, I regret to say, in spite of the fact that Wust spoke to me about him and even presented me with a photograph. But one knows enough of Scheler's history to realize that he was at once a contemplative metaphysician and *ein unruhiger Geist* and to see how strongly his line of thought would have appealed to Wust.

Man is from one point of view something belonging to Nature; he can be considered as an 'it'. But from another point of view he stands out from Nature as a being belonging to the realm of Spirit. This is to say that he is neither pure spirit nor purely infra-spiritual: he is a middle-being, between *Bios and Logos,* as Wust puts it. Originally he has a natural piety and a natural reverence towards Being as manifested in Nature and a spontaneous religion. This initial state of rest, that is, of being at home, as it were, in the world, of acceptance, of wonder at Being and reverence before Being (which on the religious level is reflected in a spontaneously religious attitude) is made possible only through spirit or mind. It may be analogous in some way to the unquestioning acceptance of animals; but it is obviously something more; it is the attitude of a being that is not simply an animal. At the same time it is mind or spirit which destroys this initial naive attitude and the initial reverence and wonder before Being. Reflection lies as a potentially dynamic element within the phenomenon of primitive naivety, and it is inevitable that it should become an active moment. For man is essentially a rest-less, promethean being; and if we say that the state of primitive naivety is the thesis, we shall have to add that it contains within itself its antithesis, the questioning of the initial reverence and piety and of all spontaneous convictions. The question is there-fore, not whether man can return to the primitive state of naivety, but whether he can reach a second naivety on a higher level. Whereas for Hegel reflection destroys for ever the primi-tive state of innocence, for Wust man can achieve under the form of 'wisdom' a second naivety. Ideally, this second stage will be characterized by faith in the personal God of theism, by reverence before the moral law and by reverence before creation as the work of God. But it is a stage won by and through reflec-tion, and though it is necessary for the fulfilment of the human personality, it is not inevitable in the case of any individual. For a man may surrender to the power of the purely negative moment of reflection, to scepticism, or he may go on to defi-ance, to the proclamation of Being as the absurd.

In *Naivität und Pietät* Wust treats of the dialectic of the human mind without explicit reference to specifically Christian doctrines, but it is clear that the book is the fruit of his own movement from the faith of his childhood through reflection to his new-found adult faith. It would be a mistake, however, to think that the value of the book is purely autobiographical. He himself draws attention to the presence of the theme in a socio-logical and historical setting in Rousseau. It was a problem with which Nietzsche struggled in a different setting. And it is a problem with which many thinkers are concerned today. Naive faith having been shattered by reflection, is it possible to ad-vance to a new faith, to what Wust calls wisdom, a faith which presupposes 'reflection'? And, if so, what is this new faith? Can man, who has eaten of the fruit of the tree of knowledge of good and evil, achieve reintegration of the personality at a higher level? One can say that Jaspers, Marcel, Aldous Huxley and other such writers were concerned with this question.

It is easily understandable that Wust's activity as a teacher left him little time for prolonged philosophical reading and reflection. He gave all the time to philosophy that could be spared while at the same time devoting himself conscientiously to his professional work. When his classes finished on a Saturday he spent the rest of the day and Sunday in reading philosophical works. But he acknowledged himself that he could never catch up, as it were; and he felt this handicap when he had become a professor of philosophy. Possibly it was a greater handicap in Germany than it would be in this country. However, he did what he could; and though his determination to pursue serious philosophical study at the same time that he was teaching in a secondary school can hardly have benefited him physically, he produced a second work during his period at Cologne, namely *Die Dialektik des Geistes* (*The Dialectic of Mind or Spirit*), which was published in 1928.

In this work Wust begins by arguing that the contemplation of nothingness as a possibility leads to the conviction that the existence of anything requires an absolute Being, a mysterious primordial will to production, concrete and eternal. It is also energy or act, and form. In determining the character of the absolute Being he proceeds from contemplation of the human spirit as relatively independent to the affirmation of God as absolute Spirit. We thus have three levels: Nature below man, man as the relatively independent spirit, a creative person, and lastly God as absolute Spirit and Creator in the full sense. Wust then turns to what he calls 'speculative anthropology', the metaphysics of man as spirit. And he argues against all those who see in man nothing more than an animal gifted with a reason which has developed to serve a vital purpose. Apart from the intrinsic difficulties of such a point of view, it neglects the super-biological region of spiritual and intellectual values, intellectual and artistic creation, and so on. No doubt, these levels have developed; but that does not alter the fact that they reveal the nature of the human person.

The fresco of the creation of Adam by Michelangelo in the Sistine Chapel is taken by Wust as a symbol of the human soul's awakening to the conscious life of the spirit. This awakening is characterized, not by doubt of reality, but by wonder and reverence, by acceptance. But the human person contains within himself the seeds of conflict. Reason, as it develops its conscious life, can identify itself with the vital urge to self-assertion and move restlessly onwards in a flight beyond all limits. Or a tension and division may develop between *Verstand* and *Vernunft*, between abstract reason and concrete intuition, leading to rationalism on the one hand or a depreciation of reason in favour of unchecked intuitions on the other. Or the will may be emphasized rather than the mind, and will, as free, is capable of defiance of the moral order and even of God Himself. Wust's point seems to be that the passage from the primitive state of naivety is inevitable if the potentialities of the human person are to be fulfilled, but that this awakening to conscious life contains within itself the root of the dialectic which any individual must be conscious of in some degree in himself.

But the dialectic is not confined to the individual as individual: it permeates the society of men. Human beings are bound together in solidarity by three media. The first is the world of expression, language, art, the objective institutions created by the human spirit. There is secondly the material scene and all the physical factors which bind human beings together in a common environment and which influence history. There is thirdly the interaction of wills. And there is action and reaction between all these factors. The material factors may initiate change, and so may the restlessness of the human will. The objective institutions created by man act as a check on the anarchy which would arise from sheer change; but at the same time their inadequacy necessitates change. Further, the dialectic of the individual's life is reflected in history. In one society the power of the reason (*der Verstand*) asserts itself, in another the urge to power, in another belief and faith. And the different types of society react on one another. In history we see man write large, as it were; naturally enough, since it is human history of which we are speaking.

It is not quite clear how far Wust admits the concept of historical progress. He certainly rejects the old-fashioned idea of rectilinear progress; but inasmuch as he believes that the goal of history is a society of persons bound together in common allegiance to the moral law and in devotion to God, it would seem that a concept of dialectical progress is required. The individual contains within himself the seeds of relative distintegration; but at the same time it is only through the development of his potentialities, which may lead to this disintegration, that he can achieve the full integration of the personality at a higher level. Similarly, it is through the changing forms of human society, each of which may be the expression of an overemphasis, that the final goal of history is approached. Whether Wust thought that it could, or would, ever be reached in this life is a question to which he does not appear to give any very clear answer in *Die Dialektik des Geistes*.

In the autumn of 1930 Wust was appointed to the chair of philosophy at Münster. Here he found himself in congenial surroundings, in a fine Catholic city, and with opportunity to devote himself exclusively to the studies that he loved most. His mind continued to turn round the problem of the spiritual restlessness of man, the problem of the *insecuritas humana,* and out of his constant meditation was born *Ungewissheit und Wagnis* (*Uncertainty and Venture*), which was published in 1937. But before saying anything about its contents I should like to relate a trivial anecdote in connection with the work.

One Thursday morning I walked with Wust to Mecklenbeck. Dr Vorholt proved to be away for the day, and we entered an inn and ordered some coffee. If I remember right, it was the innkeeper's daughter who brought the coffee. She congratulated Wust on his new book and said that she had read it with great interest. I was rather surprised at this, for it can hardly be said that Wust makes easy reading. He passed it off by telling me that the young lady had enjoyed a better education than one would naturally expect, and that she was interested in philosophical matters and liked to talk about them. Wust was obviously pleased at the incident, and I thought afterwards that his pleasure was probably largely due to the fact that in his book he had dealt with a human problem and that he was pleased to find that the problem and his treatment of it had a vital meaning for an ordinary, though naturally intelligent and reflective, fellow-being.

In the book in question Wust starts from the fact of human insecurity, understood in a quite concrete way. Apart from those who seem to love insecurity rather than security, and who appear therefore as 'exceptions', human beings are animated by the desire for security in life. But they are faced with the obvious fact that no state of affairs in this world is secure: all lies open to what may seem to be the caprice of the irrational. The same insecurity can be seen in the intellectual sphere. Men strive after certainty, after possession of the truth; yet no set of truths seems to be secure. We have simply to contemplate the history of philosophy in order to see this. An analogous insecurity makes itself felt even in the region of religion. Apart from those who have a faith which knows no shadows, faith is accompanied by a feeling of insecurity, whether it is faith in God, in revelation, or in personal salvation.

From the fact of human insecurity Wust passes to its metaphysical basis, and this he finds in man's nature as a 'middle-being'. Man partakes of nature and spirit; but he is neither completely. The animal suffers insecurity, it is true, but not as man suffers it. The animal is one, so to speak, with the stream of nature: it cannot stand apart from nature. It is at home in nature, completely part of it. In this sense it is *animal securum.* Man, however, is not completely part of nature; and he cannot be at home in nature. He is *animal insecurum.* If he strives to reduce himself to the animal level, he soon finds the difference. For his desires, unlike those of the animal, proceed to infinity. On the other hand, man is not pure spirit: he is not at home on this level either. As spirit, he can proceed from darkness into light, ignorance into knowledge; but he cannot achieve the state of vision of a pure spirit. He is a middle-being, a composite of *Bios* and *Logos*, and this is the root of his insecurity. He lacks the definiteness and fixity of the animal nature; for he is rational and free. On the other hand he lacks the final security of those who enjoy the vision of God in heaven and whose possession of the supreme good means that they cannot turn away from it.

Man's uncertainty and insecurity provides the field for venture (*Wagnis*). But this venture, this exercise of freedom, can take two forms. It can take the form of blind venture, on the supposition that the world is unintelligible. (Presumably the revolt of man as described by Camus would come under this heading.) Or man can recognize the intelligibility of reality or being, keep it before his mind, in spite of the fact that it is only partially and fragmentarily visible to him, and 'from a minimum of intellectual visibility draw a maximum of love'. Wust proceeds to consider the interplay of uncertainty and venture at the three levels of vital existence (the level of 'fortune'), of intellectual life, especially in philosophy, and of the religious life. I leave philosophy for the moment and restrict my remarks to the final level.

Wust raises the question why, after all the logical acumen and intellectual labour that have been devoted to the construction and perfecting of proofs of the existence of God, these proofs, whether taken separately or united in some way, are incapable of winning a universal assent. Human beings strive after certainty concerning the existence of God. They would like to settle the question once and for all one way or the other. They would like to be certain that God exists or that there is no God. But no such final certainty is achieved. Those who do not believe in God would say, of course, that the arguments are invalid. But the fact remains that they have appeared and do appear valid to many people who are by no means intellectual simpletons. Those who accept them may be inclined to ascribe failure to recognize their validity either to stupidity or to lack of good will. But the fact remains that the proofs are rejected by people who by no stretch of the imagination can be considered stupid, and it is not all of these who do not wish to believe in God. Some of them may be wishful thinkers in reverse, so to speak; but not all of them are. Wust's line of explanation is more or less this. All arguments for the existence of God proceed from the conviction that reality is intelligible. And most arguments proceed from the conditioned to the unconditioned, finding in the absolute Being or God the supreme principle of intelligibility. But once we have got to God we are faced with an incomprehensible abyss. Wust is far from denying the validity of the arguments. What he points out is that the Being, the existence of which is affirmed as the conclusion of the argument, is and remains incomprehensible and mysterious. Any description which may be given is inadequate and halting and raises difficulties of its own. Two paths then lie open. The reason may revolt before the incomprehensibility of the Absolute: it may either refuse to assent or it may withhold assent, remaining in uncertainty (agnosticism). On the other hand, man, bearing in mind the finitude of his intellect, may make the venture of assent, the *sacrificum intellectus*. This is not a sacrifice of the intellect in the sense that there are no good grounds for assent, but it is a sacrifice of the intellect in the sense that a man is willing to sacrifice the drive of his mind towards absolute clarity and to embrace the *docta ignorantia* of Nicholas of Cusa. And the point to be noticed is that God not only is but must always remain incomprehensible, as far as this life is concerned. It is futile to expect that we shall ever reach a stage in which the arguments for the existence of God will be so improved that they will compel the assent of all. This is impossible, precisely because they are arguments for the existence of the incomprehensible and transcendent Absolute. There is and must always remain room for personal decision.

The *insecuritas humana* is, then, above all a religious pheno-menon. It comes clearly to view in connection with knowledge of God's existence. It comes also to view in the religious life. Save in exceptional instances, response to the absolute Thou is not inevitable. God's speech to the soul may be overlooked, owing, for example, to absorption in the activities of our civilization. Even when it is recognized, it need not be listened to. For it may be heard and yet defied, varying degrees of knowledge and refusal. Again, human insecurity is seen in connection with the revelation of God to man. However many good reasons may be advanced for saying that God has revealed Himself in a particular way, insecurity and uncertainty may remain. Is this really a divine word? Is it not perhaps after all a human word? And there is the continuing insecurity and uncertainty of personal salvation. The religious man longs for the complete possession of God; but, normally speaking, there is no certainty and no security as long as life lasts. The *insecuritas humana* can be transcended, so far as it can be transcended, only in the highest stages of the mystical life. It may seem that all this is very personal to Wust, reflecting his personality and inner states. No doubt it is. But the phenomena of which Wust speaks are not confined to him, as indeed he was well aware. And I have met agnostics who had scant respect for the professional 'apologists', but who had a profound respect for Wust, even if they were not convinced by his solutions. For they saw that he knew their problems by his own experience and they felt grateful to him for taking these problems in a deeply serious spirit, instead of brushing them aside as the professional apologist is so often inclined to do.

Peter Wust died on April 3rd, 1940, after suffering for some time from cancer. And in 1946 a work of his, *Der Mensch und die Philosophie* ('Man and Philosophy'), was published post-humously. In this book he draws a sharp distinction between certainty within a mathematical system and philosophical or metaphysical certainty. Within a mathematical system we can have 'rational certitude *without* human insecurity, but in philo-sophy we have only 'rational certitude *with* human insecurity'. In other words, however good philosophical (i.e., metaphysical) arguments may be, they are always accompanied by insecurity. A number of philosophers have thought that this was only a passing phenomenon, and that if only the right method could be found metaphysics could enjoy the same sort of certainty that is found within a mathematical system. Descartes, Spinoza, Leibniz and even Kant are examples. The attempt to transform metaphysics in this way has not, however, succeeded. One can understand, then, that the failure to transform metaphysics into a quasi-mathematical science leads some philosophers (the positivists) to reject metaphysics altogether. But they neglect the fact that metaphysical reflection is born out of man's existential situation. Man seeks security; he seeks to penetrate the intelligibility of reality; he seeks 'wisdom'. And he does so precisely because he is man. The positivists are so preoccupied with philosophy as science that they lose sight of philosophy as 'wisdom'.

Philosophy is concerned with the object, with man for example, and as the philosopher contemplates the object in its intelligibility, we see the positive moment of philosophy, 'rest' and contemplation. But philosophy is also critical: it examines the very foundations of philosophy itself; it knows no limits to the field of critical examination. And here we see the negative aspect of philosophy, criticism and questioning. And these two aspects of philosophy reflect the two complementary phenomena of human existence, security, or rather the desire for security, and insecurity or restlessness. Both aspects are necessary. Philosophy without its positive aspect, which Wust calls the 'homecoming' aspect, degenerates into sheer criticism and scepticism and neglects the very goal of philosophy. But philosophy without its negative moment degenerates into dogmatism, into the passive acceptance of a fixed system, the principles of which are regarded as unquestionable. The two moments are as essential to philosophy as their analogues are in the life of man in general. In the history of philosophy we see the dialectic of the two aspects, as in human history in general we see the dialectic of the two aspects of man. 'The ultimate ground of the insecurity of philosophy as science clearly lies in the insecurity of human nature itself. The insecurity of philosophy is thus a consequence of the close connection between philosophy and the essentially insecure human being'.

It will be seen that Wust's philosophy centred upon the human person, and especially upon what he called *insecuritas humana*. To this theme he returned in his various books, considering the subject from different points of view. He believed of course that human insecurity would cease in the next life, with the full possession of God; but he regarded it as an essential phenomenon of man *in statu viatoris*. He examined the various deformations to which it may lead — defiance, scepticism, barren rationalism, and so on; but at the same time he looked on it as essential to the full development of the human personality. To take but one example, repose in one particular metaphysical system, as though it were the complete and final word, was for him a state of mental stagnation. But the restlessness of the human mind, its 'homelessness', effectually prevents the survival of this state of stagnation. On the other hand, the spirit's impulse towards being and truth acts as a check on the intellectual anarchy and scepticism which would result from the mind's restlessness if it operated alone. Both moments of the dialectic are necessary for the full development of mental life.

Does this mean that Wust regarded no truth as final or assured? This was not at all his point of view. For example, he was convinced that the human reason can know that God exists; but at the same time he was acutely aware of the mystery of the incomprehensible Godhead and of the atmosphere of uncertainty, to speak paradoxically, which this mystery may cast back on the very argument by which its existence is known. He believed firmly in the objective truth of the Catholic faith; but at the same time he realized that faith, because of the mysterious character of the object, is always a venture, a self-commitment.

Wust's chief service to philosophy in his own country was probably the help he rendered in reawakening what I may call the feeling for metaphysics and for metaphysical contemplation. He was not a system-builder, like so many other German philosophers. Nor is it likely that he will go down in the history of philosophy as a great thinker. But he helped to break through the nets of Neo-Kantianism and of positivism and to direct attention to the human person as a human person and to the openness of the human spirit to the Transcendent. And his philosophy has the merit of having grown, not out of a mere devotion to the past, but out of the dialectic of his own inner life. It is in this sense, if any, that he can be called an 'existentialist'.

I should like to close with a quotation from Wust's farewell message to his university students, dated December 18th, 1939. 'In my present time of suffering I am especially grateful to God for two things. First, for the fact that in my life He has shown me ever more clearly the truth of Christ. Secondly, for the fact that in the nine years of my work at Münster He has given me the power and the great grace of openly bearing witness to this truth in the lecture-hall. This witness was, as I know, often very difficult, because it was dangerous. But I have ventured all in the strength of grace, and I know now, *non confundar in aeternum*. And if you should ask me now, before I depart and depart finally, whether I know of a magic key which can open the final door to the wisdom of life, I should answer you "Yes". And this magic key is not reflection, as you might perhaps expect from a philosopher, but prayer. Prayer, understood as complete self-offering, makes a man tranquil, childlike, objective. For me a man grows on the level of humanity in proportion as he is able to pray — by which I mean true prayer alone. Prayer characterizes the final humility of the spirit. The great things of life are given only to the spirits that pray. But it is in suffering that one can best learn to pray'.

INDEX